ENTREPRENEUR
Success
Stories
VOLUME 3

ENTREPRENEUR
Success
Stories

VOLUME 3

How common people
achieve uncommon results

LORAL LANGEMEIER
AND JOHN C. ROBINSON

LiveOutLoud Publishing

Entrepreneur Success Stories

How Common People Achieve Uncommon Results

Volume Three

Edited by Loral Langemeier and John C. Robinson

Copyright © 2014 Loral Langemeier and John C. Robinson

For information, or to order additional copies of this book, please contact:

Live Out Loud Publishing

 is the logo for Live Out Loud Publishing.

is the logo for Live Out Loud, Inc., for which Loral Langemeier is Founder and CEO.

Phone: 707-688-2848 | Fax: 707-402-6319
Email: info@earnprofitsfromyourpassion.com

Cover and book design by Cypress House

Library of Congress Control Number: 2012406892

ISBN 978-0-9912611-0-9

Printed in the USA
1 3 5 7 9 8 6 4 2

*For Jim, a visionary pioneer
who knew the power and
potential of human resources.*

CONTENTS

Entrepreneur
Success
Stories

Volume 3

FOREWORD

My twenty-six-year career of teaching, training, coaching, mentoring, and advising more than 2,000 individuals allows me to reflect on many successes, and brings to my attention the foundations and structure needed to become successful. Guiding people in their first launch of a business requires meeting them at their present level of accomplishment and helping them move to the next level. Encouraging them to visualize their success is an important component of identifying the motivation to move to that next level. We all continually seek more than we have, and giving that pursuit a sense of direction is often the difference between success and failure. Once we develop a motivated pattern, most often the trajectory to success is within reach.

Success is an ever changing, evolving sense of fulfillment that only you the business owner can define. In this volume of *Entrepreneur Success Stories*, you'll find accounts of success as defined by thriving entrepreneurs. They describe achieving success through setting and attaining goals that yield freedom, money, and all the other results they're looking for from their businesses. The goals they set derive from their clear vision of success and their passion to accomplish that vision. In their journey, they've become masterful at running a business, masterful of the service they provide, and masterful at developing personal abilities. You'll read of their progression to mastery and how they used the intuition that arises from it to develop the next steps toward ever-greater success.

Business ownership is all about mastering yourself so as to reach your own greatest sense of fulfillment, whether it's a six-figure income, the realization of a lifelong dream of attainment, or a set of specific goals.

Here you'll read about each business owner's approach, which includes their identifying what they bring to their businesses, which areas they need to improve, and what drives them to reach their highest level of accomplishment.

Find your pattern of success by reading these stories and placing yourself in these business owners' shoes. You too will find your success and a measure of how to move forward with your business.

Pamela Patterson, CEO
West Company
"Building Better Businesses since 1988"

INTRODUCTION

Loral Langemeier

ENTREPRENEURS WORLD-WIDE HAVE experienced an unprecedented time of opportunity during the last six years. At first, this statement may not seem to make sense, especially when one considers that this time period also includes the worst recession the United States has experienced since the Great Depression. However, a closer look tells a different story.

Even the most successful investors and entrepreneurs were not left unscathed by the recent economic crisis. Many businesses failed under the pressure of dwindling prospects, declining revenue, and mounting expenses. If you are among the list of business owners that survived these turbulent times, you are to be congratulated. But I'm also excited for you, especially when I think of the many ways you stand to benefit from the persistence and faith it took to keep your doors open for business.

During the last few years, many investors, speakers, trainers, coaches, and consultants elected to abandon their dreams and return to the false security of the drudging, dreary, day-to-day experience otherwise known as "a job." Their exodus means that those businesses that survived through these lean years are now first in place to win over the consumers who will be reentering these markets.

Already, we are seeing resurgent growth in real estate markets, and the demand for speakers has skyrocketed like never before. Imagine what it may mean if your business is strategically poised to take advantage of this renewed demand for products or services that support these and similar market niches!

Now, before you start thinking that something is about to be handed to you on a silver platter, I must warn you that you still have to be prepared, you still need to do the work, and it is critical that the actions you take are chosen and sequenced properly to deliver the maximum results in exchange for your investments of time and money.

It is for this reason I am so excited to present to you the third volume in my *Entrepreneur Success Stories* series. We structured volume 1 to give you the tools and skills needed to create or expand a business and to allow you to recognize — and immediately act upon — new entrepreneurial opportunities. In volume 2 we continued the conversation by explaining the marketing and sales strategies that are necessary to create income on demand.

Unfortunately, getting your first 100 sales or your first six-figure income year may not be the ultimate entrepreneurial success you were looking for. And that is why we decided to focus volume 3 of the *Entrepreneur Success Stories* series on the missing ingredient that 98 percent of entrepreneurs lack: the strategies necessary for business growth and acceleration.

As you read through John and Ursula's chapter focusing on the principles of growth and acceleration, be sure to take lots of notes, but more importantly constantly ask yourself where you are with implementing each of the 10 activities they highlight as necessary for bringing significant, positive change to your business.

At one time, many business owners would be content with making $100,000 over a 12-month period. Today's entrepreneurs are more demanding. With the *Entrepreneur Success Stories* series, we have worked hard to bring you the stories, strategies, and winning solutions from business owners at varying levels of uncommon success, including those who are now generating over one million dollars a year.

My challenge for you is to adopt a similar mindset. For some of you, that might mean your annual income objective is still a six-figure target. However, for a growing number of you, I know your financial thermostat now includes two commas rather than one.

The good news is this: regardless of how little or how much success you've already attracted to yourself and your business, I am committed to helping you achieve your desired results. In fact, I will leave you with this single suggestion: your path to success will not be one that you travel alone.

If you have not already done so, you will want to put into place a team of people who will support you. A personal/virtual assistant could be the first person you bring on to assist you and free your time up to concentrate on revenue-producing activities. Don't forget those who will also work on your business, such as an attorney. Every agreement you enter into should be reviewed by your attorney before you sign. And finally, don't forget to think about your own exit strategy. Many entrepreneurs identify an operations manager or program director who can eventually take over the business and replace them, allowing them the freedom to start up a new entrepreneurial venture or enjoy a partial or complete retirement.

Extended teams are now driving even more entrepreneurs to faster success than ever before. This usually takes the form of strategic joint venture partnerships. Ask yourself who you could partner with this year to reach the goals you have established for yourself and your business. Just like a race horse in the Kentucky Derby, this one move alone could take you from last place to first place in your niche market in just a matter of months.

Entrepreneurial growth and acceleration is all about developing the mindset that keeps you on a perpetual fast track to success. This is your time to soar — don't miss this opportunity!

HOW TO USE THIS BOOK

John C. Robinson and Loral Langemeier

THE *ENTREPRENEUR SUCCESS STORIES* book series is a collection of examples which, taken together, form a picture of the real life of an entrepreneur. Originally, it was conceived as a single book which would stand alone in the marketplace. However, within months of launching the project, we discovered the interest in the book was far greater than Loral and I had originally envisioned. Just as with any business, we modified our original business plan to meet the new market conditions.

The *Entrepreneur Success Stories* series is now poised to bring you a virtually unlimited supply of examples illustrating how entrepreneurs just like you successfully launched a company or substantially expanded the results of an already existing business.

To begin using this book, we suggest you consult the table of contents to locate the specific chapter in which you may be most interested. For example, maybe you've encountered many obstacles in your attempts to start or grow your business. We refer to this as adversity. On your path to success, you will encounter adversity, perhaps more often than you anticipated. That is why we've included a chapter in this volume from Fred Smith, who shows us how to use resiliency to not only see us through these tough times but also to discover opportunity within adversity.

For those who like to follow a system, you may find Timothy Noonan's chapter solves many of the problems you have been facing. Timothy believes that success is all about pursuing one's passions while helping others create successful business endeavors. As he creatively lets us know what Marilyn Monroe, magic, and marketing all have in common, he also shares with us his list of the top seven success lessons you can apply to your business and life.

Perhaps you may be looking for lasting success. If so, Craig Batley shares five key strategies acquired over 40 years of entrepreneurship that will help you to be persistently productive. Give serious consideration to how you could apply each of these strategies to your own business.

Our vision was to have volume 3 exist as a stand-alone book not requiring the reader to have any prior experience with volumes 1 and 2. Although we feel we succeeded in meeting this vision, we also wanted this volume to complement the success principles revealed in the first two volumes of the *Entrepreneur Success Stories* series. Those of you who wish to explore the full magnitude of this concept should purchase volumes 1 and 2 of *Entrepreneur Success Stories* from Amazon (Kindle versions are now available for your convenience). You can then review volume 1 to learn how to recognize an entrepreneurial opportunity and act on it immediately; and volume 2 will help you learn how to drive income to the bottom line of your business through super-successful sales and marketing strategies.

This installment of *Entrepreneur Success Stories* is intended to meet you wherever you are on your journey as an entrepreneur. Its purpose is to help you discover and build an implementable plan to achieve substantial growth and acceleration in your business in the shortest amount of time possible.

As with all books in the *Entrepreneur Success Stories* series, this book can easily be used as a daily learning exercise. Spend 30 minutes with it each day, and read one chapter two or three times to identify its primary message. Ask yourself what you learned from the chapter and how it can be applied to your life or business.

While it is tempting to think of the impact one could have if one were a Hollywood celebrity, many of us pass such fantasies off as unattainable pipe dreams. But what if there were a way you could become a celebrity in your own community? Well, there is, and Mary Lou Luebbe-Gearhart's chapter shows you how to do that while creating success for your business.

Much of what we do as business owners to expand our business, create greater profits, help more people, and give ourselves more time to spend with our own friends and family will rely on the decisions we make. Have you ever noticed how we tend to second-guess ourselves on nearly every decision we make, oftentimes making wrong decisions when we knew we should have done something different? Worse yet, we may not make any decision at all, because we are too confused to act. If this is where you are stuck, you may find Sandra Harris' chapter on Instinctive Leadership will help you to more effectively create success in your business simply by trusting and leveraging your intuition.

Ursula Mentjes and John C. Robinson spent several months comparing notes about their own successes as well as other influential entrepreneurs they've partnered with. Their result, the chapter on the principles of entrepreneurial growth and acceleration, is applicable to all readers, but especially those who desire to reach their full potential in a relatively short period of time. This chapter is featured on the following pages and we encourage you to read it first. To the core list of success principles identified by John and Ursula, ask yourself what additional ideas shared by each of the contributing entrepreneurs included in this book could be added to the goals and objectives you have for your business.

The end result of this process will be the outline of your own customized plan for success. This outline will include what John Robinson frequently refers to as "the pieces of the puzzle." Putting your puzzle together, and identifying that one piece which is the key to your overall success, is the next step. As you begin that journey, remember that we are here to help. Share your own story of uncommon success or write to us about your experiences at alumnisuccess@liveoutloud.com. Let us know how you attracted triumphant results in your own business.

The format of this book is easy to follow. The length of each chapter is designed to be read in a single sitting so that the primary message from each story can be quickly understood and applied to your own circumstances. Note that each contributor's name is provided at the beginning of his or her respective chapter. Many of the contributors are graduates of Loral's Big Table. These alumni have taken the time to share their expertise with you, and we encourage you to learn from the success they've created in their businesses. The Big Table number that follows their name identifies the graduates, as in John C. Robinson (LBT #10).

THE PRINCIPLES OF ENTREPRENEURIAL GROWTH AND ACCELERATION

John C. Robinson and Ursula Mentjes

WHAT'S THAT? You just opened your business banking account statement and your balance is still stuck at the same level it's been for the past 17 months? How frustrating!

If the above story rings true for you, or even if you've seen your bank account balance gradually declining month after month, then you have probably been looking for effective strategies that can grow and accelerate the success of your business.

It's likely you've already tried a few things. Maybe you started with social media: establishing a personal profile, garnering a few likes, and hoping some of them visit your website. Still no change in the back account.

Before long, you may have decided to purchase 10,000 leads from a list broker. A single email blast to the entire list — certainly, that's a way to boost sales. Right?

Then you likely heard about Search Engine Optimization (SEO). One consultant later and $3,000 poorer, there's still no measurable increase in the number of your opt-ins and, even worse, no way to confidently tie the few sales you did make back to any of your recent efforts.

Bottom-line assessment: three months of focused labor, no measurable increase in income to show for it.

Regardless of where you are in this recurring monthly cycle of juggling bills, searching for zero-interest credit cards, or making loans to your company to cover the disproportionate excess of business expenses compared to cash flow, the last thing we want you to consider is quitting.

What many of us in this situation don't realize is that the small business which we had the courage to create in the first place is also our ticket to freedom, allowing us to escape from the rat race and the accompanying feeling of lack and limitation that may have invaded our thoughts from time to time — or all the time.

But how do we unlock the potential hidden within our own business? In this chapter, Ursula and I would like to share with you 10 principles for entrepreneurial growth and acceleration. We encourage you to read and study them, then create a plan for incorporating them into your daily activities over the next 90 days.

▪ JUST DREAMING VERSUS DARING TO DREAM BIG

So many things we take for granted today (e.g., cars, fax machines, cell phones, or even pens and pencils) all started as a dream.

Dreaming about greater wealth, abundance, or success is nothing new. All of us have done it, most likely more than once. However, the majority of us have run up against a common limitation: the lack of results.

Perhaps this scenario is all too familiar to you:

- ◆ We dream about something we want to have or accomplish.

- ◆ We might even attend a webinar or seminar to learn more about how to acquire or accomplish the subject of our dreams.

- ◆ Fueled by the excitement of the seminar's motivational speakers, or simply by our hope that a positive outcome will result in a relatively short period of time, we decide to "try it for a while"...

- ◆ ... and, as in the fictitious example that opened this chapter, we see no success after making a considerable investment of time and money.

* Other "influential" people in our life then tell us to stop dreaming, or to "get a job" assuming we don't already have one.

* Humbled by our lack of results, we return our focus back to the job, until a few months later — we have another dream, and the cycle starts anew.

Obviously, many of the successful entrepreneurs we know have broken out of this cycle and continue to attract increasingly greater amounts of wealth and abundance. What is it they have that others lack? The answer to this question comes in three parts.

Part 1 is simply unleashing the power of our dreams. Rather than just dreaming, you should be willing to Dream Big — and then to give yourself permission to do so! Here's an example of how John Robinson dared to dream big: one day, while looking at all the books on the shelf in the store of a national book retail chain, he suddenly asked himself, "Why can't I have my own book on this shelf?" Although John had never before written a book and had no idea how the book publishing industry worked, he began work on his novel the very next day.

Part 2 is tapping into the burning desire necessary to propel you into action in pursuit of your dream. John's burning desire was quite simple; as a young African-American male growing up in an impoverished section of Pittsburgh, Pennsylvania, he knew that successfully publishing a book would open up many doors of opportunity for him — the same doors of opportunity that had been closed for generations to others in his community. We reveal more about the power of desire later in this chapter.

Part 3 is applying a process that allows you to win; not just win once or twice, but win consistently. Think, for a moment, of the successful entrepreneurs or gurus you know or may have met. They, too, are using this process to create their success. The initial parts of this process are incorporated into the remaining sections of this chapter.

But first, we must ask YOU some important questions. What is your Dream? And, more importantly, are you Dreaming Big? We encourage you to create the image in your mind that succinctly describes you and your business as a champion. Take a moment to write it down. In fact, do it now while the challenge is fresh in your mind. For example, you might write something like, "My company is the leading North American provider of books, videos, and personal services for dog and cat owners in search of quick, effective, and easy-to-learn solutions for training their pet." This image will become the core foundation of your big dream, so be sure to spend a few minutes right now and describe your champion's image as specifically as you possibly can.

Next, create a short mantra you can say out loud to yourself, over and over. For example, when John Robinson created his "One Thousand Dollars a Day for 100 Days in a Row" program many years ago, he used the name of the program (shown in quotations above) as a mantra he repeated to himself hundreds of times each day. Now, whenever any doubt, fear, or worry begins to enter your mind, simply repeat your mantra over and over. Doing this enough times on a repeated basis will allow you to become your Dream (Oh, yes, after 100 consecutive days, John exceeded his goal of $100K in 100 days.).

■ THE "ZONE": LIVING THE DREAM

When people watch Michael Jordan or Lebron James shoot hoops with limitless ease and grace, cutting through their opponents' defenses like a knife through butter, they often describe those players as being "in the zone." Those athletes' beliefs in themselves and their abilities appear superhuman to us.

But, was it always this way? For many of us, entering this zone can be one of the most complicated things we do. So let's break it down into its component steps.

Step 1 is simply recognizing that your Dream might be something you've never accomplished before. Allow yourself to become excited by this circumstance instead of being overwhelmed by doubt. For instance, although John had never before written a book, he allowed himself to be excited by his dream of being a published author rather than dwelling on stories of others who had tried something similar and failed.

As another example, Ursula's big dream was to become president of the multi-million dollar company she was working for.

Step 2 involves thinking like a child again. Children approach almost anything with a persistent desire to succeed. More important, however, is their willingness to blindly take that first step. Although many of us can't remember when we took our first step, it's probably safe to assume we fell down a few times before learning how to walk. The key is recognizing that we did take that first step. Being willing to take the first step in your business or towards that Big Dream you have allows you to move that much closer to a successful outcome.

In Ursula's case, she went from being a sales professional to being the president — because she stayed focused on her dream. Using persistence as a guide, she learned how to successfully sell millions of dollars in computer training and then lead teams of sales professionals to do the same. Five years later, at the age of 27, she became president of her company!

Step 3 involves recognizing that success may come in many forms. We should welcome success in whatever form it decides to take with us. When John finished writing his book, he believed there was only one method, involving several discrete steps, whereby a writer could publish his or her book. He repeatedly made several attempts to follow these exact steps over several months, but each attempt failed. It was only when John was willing to accept the idea that success could come to him in forms previously unimagined, that things began to change. He embraced the words of his mentor, who had told him about the process of self-publishing. Within 90 days of that conversation, John brought to market his first two self-published books. One of them went on to sell over 108,000 copies at an international level.

John's story is probably applicable to many aspiring writers. The belief that "I'll never be a published author" can be firmly entrenched in your mind if you've not even started to write your first book yet, or you have 25 rejection letters in response to your book proposal. But what about that copy editor who offered to donate two hours of his time to show you how to write an opening chapter that would mesmerize your readers — why haven't you ever followed up with him? Or perhaps you need to attend that "Self-publishing on Kindle" workshop that is happening next weekend?

Ah, you see? Perhaps now you're beginning to understand how and why success can appear to you in so many different forms. It is with this understanding that entrepreneurial growth and acceleration truly begins to manifest itself in your business.

Entering the zone and living our Dream is not hard. Once learned, the process can be invoked quickly and at any time. Here are some ways to get started:

1. Write a one-sentence vision statement for yourself, beginning with the words "I AM. . ."

2. Have a positive, inspirational mantra you say repeatedly to yourself throughout the day (we showed you how to create this mantra earlier in this chapter).

3. Dress the part. If you want to be a six-figure business coach, make a habit of wearing your business or business casual wardrobe whenever you leave the house, even if it's just to make a deposit into your bank account. In fact, when coaching your clients from the comfort of your home office, try wearing your business suit, tie, and shoes. The energy boost that comes from that one simple behavior will instantly be felt and appreciated by your clients over the phone even though they cannot see you!

4. Tell the world. Share your vision on your blog or social media business page, and with your business coach and other business colleagues who have agreed to be your accountability partners. When our commitments are made public we feel a stronger urge to honor them.

5. Always begin your journey with the end in mind. Starting with

"what I want" is always more powerful than "what I think I might be able to do." Failing to honor and respect this single strategy is like giving yourself a severe handicap even before the race has begun.

6. Train yourself to see the words, phrases, and thoughts that have kept you stuck in the past; and replace them with the vision, mantra, and positive behaviors listed above.

THE POWER OF DESIRE

Simply put, "Desire" is a dish best shared with others.

We prepare this dish by first defining, understanding, and connecting with our purpose in life. The desire inherent in this process fuels our vision, allowing us to enter the zone and begin living our Dream in the most positive, energetic manner. With our desire and vision in place, we are ready to take a critical step towards our success: sharing our desire and view of success with a team of individuals we strategically surround ourselves with. This team, if formed correctly, will consist of individuals who are smarter than us.

With the leadership you bring to the equation, your team has the potential to become one of the most powerful elements in your business.

Unfortunately, the power of desire is rarely leveraged properly in a business. This might happen because the business owner never creates the big vision or shares it with his or her team. In other instances, the team members may not be qualified to achieve the goals necessary to implement the vision. When this happens, it may be time to attract new members to your team. Remember, you must put your ego aside and attract the people whose skills and talents in key areas surpass your own. In effect, they should challenge you to grow.

WHO WIELDS THE HAMMER IN YOUR BUSINESS?

The tasks in your business are many: social media, website design, accounting and bookkeeping, marketing campaigns, joint ventures, affiliate management, sales, customer service, printing business cards, responding to emails, shopping cart management, updating autoresponders, tax preparation, etc. Take some time to create a list of all the various activities you perform in your business. Don't be surprised if the list is surprisingly long. Many entrepreneurs fall into the trap of taking on more than they have time to do.

For some of us, this may simply result from a tendency to become distracted by new, shiny objects. However, for an even greater number of entrepreneurs, the real motivation is the perception that, by doing all these things ourselves, we as business owners can cut costs and increase net profits. What many of us don't realize is that allowing our time to be consumed by a mountain of administrative minutiae actually places a stranglehold on our company's ability to generate more sales and grow quickly.

If you are wielding the proverbial hammer in your business, you should get in the habit of asking yourself at frequent intervals the following question: "Is what I am doing right now the best use of my time?" Whenever the answer is "No," challenge yourself to seek out the people who could do these tasks for you.

One complaint we often hear is, "I can't afford to hire the people I need to do all these tasks." Yet we see business owners spending 10 hours coding a website when they could have hired that task out to a Web designer who could have accomplished the same project in less than 90 minutes.

As leaders of our business, we must recognize that there is always someone who can swing the hammer ten times better than we can. As one of our mentors once said, "If you're the smartest person in the room, you are in the wrong room." As leaders, our job is to put our financial projections in place, create sales targets that will stretch us to do more, and build the team today for the business we want tomorrow.

■ TAP INTO THE "WHY" — THE "HOW" WILL COME LATER

"But how do I do that?" Yes, we know that may be a question going round in your head right now as you think about *how to build a team today for the business you want tomorrow.* Our advice: take a deep breath and relax.

You see, the quickest way to stall your forward progress is to get stuck in the "how." *How will I hire my team? Should I bring them on full-time or part-time? As employees or contractors? At what pay rate? How do I create a position description?*

Rather than devote your thoughts and energy to such an endless array of questions, use your vision of success to focus on your desire to fulfill your purpose. As a result, your wants and needs will become more clearly defined and, in turn, the "how" tends to sort itself out during the process. As you boldly take each step forward, everything you will need at that stage will reveal itself to you.

Finally, as you examine your visions and goals, make sure they are realistic and practically attainable. How do you eat an elephant? One bite at a time. This might mean that your plan to reach $2 million of income is expanded from a 1-year to a 3-year plan, with your initial 12-month income target set at $250,000. By breaking our forward progress down into bite-sized pieces in this way, we create believable stretch targets that motivate us to get out of bed each morning and allow us to always focus on the actions necessary to reach the goal. We can't afford the anxiety that comes from outpacing ourselves or trying to manage unrealistic expectations.

■ ON BEING SAVVY AND CREATING NONLINEAR SUCCESS

When you visit some South American countries like Ecuador, the amount you pay for items from street merchants and gift shops is frequently the result of a back-and-forth negotiation between you and the store owner. You can (and should) apply this same mentality to how you run your business.

Ursula once described herself as the "Barter Queen," and John donated in-kind services in exchange for receiving his first website. That website led to more than a half million dollars in sales.

Can't afford the team members you want? Why not hire them part-time instead of full-time, rather than give up on them altogether? Likewise, why use an insufficient capital raise as the reason why you call off the international workshop you've always wanted to hold when you can attract in-kind sponsorships necessary for the workshop's success? Become your own barter queen (or king). Become savvy, and challenge yourself with the following new belief: *Anything I want can be actualized.*

Big corporations spend hundreds of thousands, if not millions, of dollars on the marketing of a single product. Obviously we don't always have the luxury of acting like a big corporation, but we can become very strategic in our thinking and in the people with whom we associate. In fact, our success in business and in life can be streamlined simply by allowing ourselves to be mentored by people who are playing a bigger and better game than we are. Imagine, for example, the entrepreneur making $65,000 per year who is now being mentored by his six-figure coach; or the entrepreneur with an income of $250,000 who is being mentored by her seven-figure coach. Emulating success in this way allows you to reach your end game a lot quicker and in a nonlinear way (i.e., in fewer steps or less time), compared to the traditional approach of working harder and putting in more hours.

▓ IS SILVER WHERE YOU WANT TO BE?

Anyone who has spent time watching the Olympics knows there are three medals given in each competitive event: gold, silver, and bronze. Many people believe someone who has placed second in an event (earning a silver medal) has done quite well for himself. When you have the opportunity to get to know the mind of a true champion however, you will realize they equate finishing second with not being good enough. Their mentality is to do whatever it takes to finish first.

As the leader of your business, you must decide if finishing second and earning a silver medal is acceptable. If not, ask yourself, "How can I show up as I've never shown up before in my life?"

This is where the opportunity to invest in yourself or your business may manifest itself. Maybe there's a personnel management or sales conference you'd like to enroll in to improve your leadership qualities. We encourage you to set a budget for opportunities like these, but always remember one thing: regardless of whether you are investing money into your business or in yourself, don't just do it to go through the motions of taking a training program. Instead, we recommend you document in writing how you plan to get a tenfold return on any business or personal development program you purchase.

▣ PRACTICING ADAPTIVE MANAGEMENT

One of the mistakes we've seen many entrepreneurs make is simply not moving fast enough. The only thing more frustrating than missing out on a great business opportunity is realizing you had advance knowledge about the opportunity but failed to act in time to take advantage of it.

One of the ways to ensure this doesn't happen to you is to put an adaptive management plan in place for your business. This could be something as simple as a monthly or quarterly meeting with your CPA or a weekly strategy session with your senior team members, each of whom delivers a report on the status of all the projects he or she is working on.

Any plan, however, is only as good as its implementation strategy. If you place adaptive management measures to work for you in your business, be sure you and your team members are ready to act decisively on the information the plan gives you. For example, when you see something that is working well or better than expected, be sure to immediately shift resources around so you can capitalize on that. John's current best-selling product, "Webinar Graduate School," came to him during a waking dream in early June 2012. Likewise, Ursula took a three-day program, "Selling with Intention," and has used what she gained there to transform everything she does in her business. Great ideas oftentimes come out of necessity and become our golden discoveries. Don't overlook, under-appreciate, or ignore them.

▓ REFERRAL-BASED MARKETING

Does a million dollars of income in eight months sound unrealistic? Well, it's actually been done, and Ursula and I know many entrepreneurs who have met or exceeded this standard. One of the common elements that contributed to their success is what we call referral-based marketing.

To understand referral-based marketing, you must first be able to clearly articulate what it is you do, who you do it for, the unique benefits your clients receive from you, and what your fees are. Put it all together into a statement you could deliver to a potential business partner in three minutes or less.

Next, make a list of everyone you know who would be receptive to receiving a call from you explaining how they can make money with your business opportunity in exchange for a very little investment of their time. Now, imagine what would happen if all these people began referring prospects they know to you. What would you offer in exchange for all those business opportunities? This is where you and your referral partner must reach agreement on a commission you will pay for each lead sent your way that turns into a paying customer. Make sure this agreement is documented in writing and signed and dated by both of you.

Referral-based marketing may result in a conversion rate of up to 90 percent. The reason it can be so successful is because the potential customers being referred to you are not cold prospects. Your referral partner is transferring the credibility and trust his clients already have in him over to you simply by making the referral. Properly executed, there are few other strategies that have as much potential to deliver to you a constant stream of warm prospects from a multitude of sources.

▓ THE FORTUNE IS IN THE . . .

But before we become too ecstatic about the success we might have with our marketing efforts, let us warn you that a high percentage of potential customers do not purchase after your first sales presentation or sales call. Unfortunately, most entrepreneurs interpret this failure to convert as a sign the prospect has said "No" to their opportunity; and they never *follow up*.

On some of our most recent product launches, we have discovered that 60–75 percent of our clients made the decision to purchase during one of our follow-up calls. If you have yet to develop a consistent and effective follow-up strategy in your business, you are leaving a lot of money on the table.

Here are some thoughts on how to avoid this problem:

1. Train your mind to think differently when you hear the word "No." When a prospect says "No" to your business opportunity, what if you were to always interpret it to mean "Not yet"? Do you see how thinking like this immediately launches you into "follow-up mode" during the sales call? If you practice this, you will find yourself seamlessly entering a conversation for setting the date and time of the next call you plan to have with the prospect.

2. If sales is something you dislike or are afraid to do, commit yourself to take training to overcome that problem or bring someone into your company who enjoys the sales process and is in alignment with your vision.

3. Share your follow-up strategy with all your team members. Remember, your prospects and clients may interact with several different people on your team each week or month. During those calls, all of your team members should have the training, ability, and comfort level to enter a basic sales/follow-up conversation as needed with your prospects and clients. This is an effective way to spark an explosive growth in sales in your business!

▦ IN CONCLUSION . . .

Don't stop. That's right — whatever you do, don't let these final paragraphs become the last time you ever look at or contemplate the strategies revealed to you on the preceding pages. Think of this moment, not as the end, but as the beginning of your entrepreneurial growth and acceleration.

At the beginning of this chapter we challenged you to create a 90-day Implementation Plan around the ten growth and acceleration principles listed above. It is now time for you to meet that challenge!

Are you willing to explore your Purpose and discover your Desire? Are you willing to Dream Big — and then to give yourself permission to do just that? Are you willing to enter the zone and begin living your dream? To support yourself in these efforts, what is your champion's image?

Each of the 10 principles listed above are exercises we hope you will return to frequently. Share the results of your thinking associated with these exercises with your senior team, your Master Mind group, and your coach or mentor. Use these connections to not only hold you accountable but to launch you on a nonlinear, accelerated path to success!

Meet the Contributors

JOHN C. ROBINSON is an award-winning author and an in-demand speaker who has shared the stage with the top business development speakers and financial strategists of our generation. In 1979, John discovered his passion for the world of birds, nature, and the outdoors. Since then he has written and/or published 12 books, become a two-time best-selling author, led clients on natural history tours around the world, and authored a computer program for nature-based software that has sold hundreds of thousands of copies (www.onmymountain.com).

Contact him at www.earnprofitsfromyourpassion.com.

URSULA MENTJES is the best-selling author of *Selling with Intention* and *One Great Goal*. She is a sales expert, Certified Sales Coach, and motivational speaker who specializes in Neuro-Linguistic Programming (NLP) to help her clients reach their highest potential in their careers and businesses. Specifically, she has helped businesses double and triple their sales revenue in as little as two months.

Ursula honed her skills at an international technical training company, starting her career in sales in 1996 and advancing to the position of president in 2001. When she was just 27 years of age, working at a company with annual revenue in the tens of millions, she was responsible for increasing sales by 90 percent in just one year. Ursula attributes her success to setting stretch goals and empowering her employees to be the best that they could be. She is passionate about helping individuals and businesses reach their full potential, so in May 2004 she founded her own professional coaching and consulting firm that specializes in working with entrepreneurs and sales professionals.

Ursula also holds a bachelor of arts degree in psychology and communication from St. Olaf College and a master of science degree in psychology from California Baptist University. She is a Certified NLP Coach through the NLP Institute of California and a 2006 graduate of Leadership California. Ursula is also president of the National Association of Women Business Owners of California. She has shared the stage with best-selling authors Loral Langemeier and Tom Antion, Giuliana Rancic and many others!

If you desire more intensive training or support, please contact Ursula at www.salescoachnow.com

YOUR PLATFORM: THE SECRET TO YOUR EVERLASTING SUCCESS

John C. Robinson

AS A BUSINESS COACH, I see so many entrepreneurs fall into the trap of waiting until everything is just right, until all the books have been written, until all the products have been created, until everything is just perfect — before they begin to market their business. This can be one of the costliest mistakes you can make in your business.

This chapter presents a simple technique that can not only help you avoid this problem, but also enable you to earn cash fast at the same time. The idea is very simple: you must have a platform, and you must have a way of communicating that platform to others.

We learn by example. So, here is one example from my business. When people meet me for the first time, I am often asked, "What does your business offer?"

In response, I usually say, "We help entrepreneurial authors and creators of information products unlock the hidden sources of income in their business."

The above statement is what we call an elevator speech. Note how it is succinctly communicated (takes me less than six seconds to say it), instantly piques the curiosity of the listener, and is designed to prompt the listener to ask a simple question — something like, "Oh, really, how do you do that?"

In most cases, that's the type of response I get, and that response allows me to speak about my platform, which I introduce as a four-part recipe:

- ✦ We start by helping our clients to **tap into their Burning Desire and use it as a source of inspiration as they identify their Greatest Skill Sets.**

- ✦ We then use a series of introspective questions to help our clients **determine what it is they know about these skills that can be transformed into Something of Value.**

- ✦ We show them how they can **create an Information Product around that value** in as little as 60 minutes.

- ✦ And finally we help our clients **integrate those Information Products back into their existing business (or a new business) to spawn unlimited streams of revenue.**

The boldface text above is my platform. The goal of this chapter is to help you create your platform.

▉ CREATING YOUR PLATFORM

The one question I get asked more than any other when teaching my students how to create their platform is this: "What is the first thing I need to do?" You might even have the same question right now as you read this chapter.

To begin creating your own platform, ask yourself: "What is the single most important benefit my customers receive from me, and why is it important to them?" Once you have identified your single most important benefit (and the reason why it's most important), take a few moments to identify the basic steps of how you deliver this benefit to your customers.

If you are a trainer who specializes in showing business owners how to generate $100,000 or more each year from social media, list the basic steps you take to accomplish this. Likewise, if you're an in-demand tax strategist who specializes in minimizing or eliminating tax liability for high-net-worth clients, identify the key strategies you use to achieve these results.

The key message here is simply this: take the greatest benefit you deliver to your clients and distill the steps necessary for your clients to realize this benefit into a set of discrete tasks that can be easily communicated to any of your prospects.

I was once in an audience listening to a trainer explain how he helped his clients become speakers capable of generating at least $1 million dollars a year. As I listened to the steps he told us anyone in the audience could follow to achieve this worthy goal, I knew right away he was delivering his platform to us.

▦ WHAT CAN YOU DO WITH YOUR PLATFORM

Many entrepreneurs never build their platform because they don't believe it will work (that's a problem with vision or confidence) or because they don't know how they could leverage their platform into something useful within their business.

Although we don't have space in this chapter to address vision or confidence in depth, please bear in mind that many of the past and present contributing authors to the *Entrepreneur Success Stories* books have written about how to attract greater confidence and extreme clarity of vision. Therefore, I will concentrate on some of the amazing things that can be done with your platform once you develop it.

Once your platform has been developed, you can use it:

* As the framework of your new book (Presell the book based on what's in it and the benefit it delivers.)

* As the framework of your next teleseminar or webinar (Presell the online course before you've completed the class lessons!)

* As the outline of your next keynote speech (Yes, you can get paid to speak even before you've published your first book or conducted your first webinar.)

♦ As the central focus for your press kit, news releases, website copy, radio or TV interview, social media presence, or other venue where you have the opportunity to create a consistent brand message about you and your business

■ TESTING YOUR PLATFORM

Your platform will likely not be created overnight, and in fact we encourage you to have patience as you develop it. It will take time to grow, to evolve, and to become seamlessly integrated with you and your business plan. You should take advantage of this time to continually test your platform. Use it in news releases, on web sites, in social media posts, on landing pages as an encouragement for prospects to opt in to your list, or even as the core message of a keynote speech you deliver.

Each time you test your platform, measure your results. How many people were exposed to your message? Of those, how many expressed some interest by opting in to your list or making some other form of contact with you? Asking yourself these and similar questions will enable you to determine whether your platform needs refinement. Keep the parts of your platform that work best in terms of attracting people's interest, and toss those elements that don't perform. In time, your platform will be concise yet powerful, and capable of attracting and holding the interest of a large number of prospects even if they are seeing you for the very first time.

In one of my businesses, I work with environmental educators and corporate partners to help introduce minority and inner city children to nature and the outdoors. There are five key steps I take to deliver my message to the school kids; I can teach these same methods to environmental educators all over the world. These five steps constitute my platform. A full 18 months before my book appeared in print, I was using this platform to deliver keynote speeches and accepting cash, checks, and credit cards for pre-orders for the book that grew out of it.

■ MONETIZING YOUR PLATFORM

Once the initial outline of your platform has been created, you are faced with an important decision: *do I launch what I have right now, or do I keep refining until I perfect it?*

My advice to you: always go for the launch sooner rather than later. It may not be perfect, but you can refine it based on the feedback you get from your initial wave of prospects. Also, doing it this way allows you to place yourself in front of an even larger audience with a marketing message that has a greater chance for success.

Unfortunately, many of the clients who I work with chose at the beginning not to monetize their platform, but instead to keep planning and perfecting it. As you might guess, this becomes one of the primary focal points of my coaching with them over the next several months. Why? Because choosing not to launch and promote your platform until it is "just right" could cost you months, years, or even decades of lost revenue.

Remember, your platform becomes the talking points for you and your business. It brands your message and, if properly created, attracts customers and business partners to your opportunity and your work.

The question is very simple: when will you ask for the cash? I recommend you start today! And when you do, incorporate the key talking points of your platform into the conversation. Your platform becomes the gateway to your everlasting success. Allow it to grow and evolve with everything that you do.

INSTINCTIVE LEADERSHIP: CREATING SUCCESS BY LEVERAGING YOUR INTUITION

Sandra Rodriguez Harris, MS, PT (LBT #87)

IF WE CALL OURSELVES ENTREPRENEURS, at some point each of us has come face to face with our intuition. By the way, how did that meeting go? What did you take away from it?

For many of us, the keys to our success have been with us all along. Yet, time and time again, when the keys are dangled in front of us we don't act! We don't trust ourselves to move forward. Why is that?

On the stage we call Life, how many times must we reenact the scene with that familiar cast of characters — *Doubt, Fear,* and *Worry?* How many times will we run from the shadow of "what other people might think"? As entrepreneurs, we've heard more than once that we must learn to trust our intuition. But how do we do that while still positioning ourselves as a leader in our company?

Just recently, I was approached by a dear friend and fellow keynote speaker who proposed to interview me to learn how I have created a lifetime of success simply by trusting my natural instinct. I'd like to share with you the results of that interview, so that you can apply them in your own business.

■ THE POWER OF NETWORKING

Although my intuitive skills were definitely at play when I was in high school, it wasn't until college that I really began to apply them. Let's begin first, though, with the end result.

The end result is that I decided to get a job in the dean's office at my college. This effectively created a virtual colleague-like relationship with my professors and with the dean. I saw my time at college as mini-training for real life. I figured if I could navigate the university system and be someone of consequence there, then this would benefit me upon graduation and during my entry into the "real world."

During this journey, I became a Student Ambassador and a Student Orientation Leader. In these formative years, I realized the path to success was not that hard. If I essentially did a little bit more than everyone else, and if I did that consistently, it would make me stand out and place me in the top 10 percent of my peers. This is a method any of you can apply now in your own business and market niche.

So, now that you've seen the end result, you might be asking, "Sandra, how did you get there?"

Great question! My intuition told me that if I followed and observed what the leaders in my business were doing, and if I did what they suggested, then my path to success would be simpler. This is what led me to apply for that job in the dean's office; and when it was suggested by one of my mentors that I become a Student Ambassador, I just did it because I knew my mentors were sharing with me strategies that had helped them become successful.

Fast forward now to graduate school: in my field, only 1 in 300 applicants usually gets accepted to the graduate school I chose to enter, and even then I was only bringing forward a 3.00 GPA from my undergraduate years — which is nothing spectacular, as I quickly learned. However, acceptance into many competitive graduate schools hinges on the ability to amass a collection of good recommendation letters. If you're connecting the dots at this point, you can imagine how the professors and the dean's office from my undergraduate school were more than willing to support my continuing education, and you can probably imagine how my recommendation letters stood apart from many other applicants simply by virtue of the people who wrote them and the positions they held.

I was fortunate, therefore, to learn the power of networking at a very young age. And I wish to emphasize one last time that the thing that drove me to begin networking was simply following my intuition and answering this question: "How can I put myself in close association with the very people I want to follow?" Remember, being in proximity to the people of influence in your niche market is what will help you get to the next level.

▨ ENTREPRENEURIAL CHESS: POSITIONING FOR SUCCESS

Success doesn't just happen. It's the result of a well-defined sequence of steps that you perform for very specific reasons and at designated points in time. I discovered that a great way to influence my success is to "project" the position(s) I need to occupy to fulfill my goal. Put another way: if I know that in three years I want to be THERE (regardless of where "THERE" is or what it means), then I ask myself, *"How do I position myself NOW to get THERE?"* More specifically, who do I need to meet, where do I need to go, what (or who) do I need to be in association with, what groups do I need to join?

Like the top performers in nearly any sport you care to mention, positioning is like seeing in your mind the moves you *know* your opponent will make even before he or she makes them. When approached in this manner, positioning and networking will become essential tools that will help you to unleash your intuition.

▨ THE ROADBLOCK

With the above foundation in place, we can now return to our infamous cast of characters: *Doubt, Fear,* and *Worry.* Why are they still on your stage? Obviously, if it was so easy to follow our intuition and discover our path to success, then everyone would be doing it. So what stops so many of us? The doubt? The fear? The unwillingness to allow ourselves to be led by our intuition?

I'd like to help you remove these roadblocks by sharing with you a process I use to act *quickly* and with confidence on my intuition. It starts with being willing to listen to your intuition and to allow it to drive your actions and influence your results. For example, when my intuition is in high gear, that gut instinct goes immediately to my head, and my brain starts processing it by asking, "How am I going to do it? How am I going to do it?" This processing continues, amidst *excitement and fear*, and it immediately leads into action, which I then carry through.

Where most people get stuck is that part about the excitement and fear. The fear represents the new adventure we are about to take. The excitement is what can incite us to take action, because we can't wait to see how it turns out. It's when you allow the fear, the self-doubt, or the worry about what others will say to overshadow your excitement — that's when you get stuck and see no progress.

Fortunately, getting unstuck is simply about trusting the process and knowing that if you take no action, no results will manifest. But if you trust the process and are willing to at least take that first step, you give yourself the opportunity to see your first result. This first result strengthens your belief and confidence, and as you take your second step, even more results will appear. For even greater results, simply continue the process — don't give up!

■ PERSISTENCE AKA STICK-TO-IT-IVENESS

And that brings us to my last main point, which is to practice what many people call "persistence." My term for this, however, is "stick-to-it-iveness." Whatever you call it, I regard this as a true character trait of successful entrepreneurs. It's so wimpy when people stop at the first sign of an obstacle! Persistent entrepreneurs, in contrast, simply keep trying; they ask for help, or they quickly figure out how to redirect their efforts into something related but more profitable. They are never done with learning!

■ FINAL GUIDELINES FOR UNLEASHING YOUR INTUITION

Here are some final thoughts, ideas, and conceptual principles I encourage you to practice regularly as you follow your own intuition:

- **Anyone can follow their passion — successful entrepreneurs turn it into a business.** Doing your passion, whatever that is, doesn't by itself guarantee success. You still must bring business sense to the table. That requires the ability to communicate, sell, and market your passion. The way you do this is with "Team."

- **There are teams and then there are "Teams."** Craigslist, guru. com, or elance.com are familiar to nearly any entrepreneur looking for a new Team member. I challenge you, however, to think differently and ask for the best! For example, rather than hire an affordable marketing consultant, why not ask the question, "How can I partner with a marketing team that has a track record of helping its clients earn at least one million dollars?"

- **Avoid the trap of "linear thinking."** Asking questions like the one above is how you avoid linear thinking; it's essentially how many successful entrepreneurs have gone from Step A to Step M, while avoiding all the intervening steps along the way. Most entrepreneurs follow the linear model. Be open to the ideas that non-linear thinking can bring to your business!

- **Define and honor your values.** In my business, I always ask myself first how I can help others or how I can serve, BEFORE I ask anyone to be my customer. And I would never expect anyone to give me money for a service if I had not invested money in myself first to make me capable of delivering that service. These are some of my values. I encourage you to define your own values — and to honor them.

- **Success does not come without its failures.** You will without doubt encounter one or more failures on your path to success. Know that they will happen, and take the time to learn from them. Even

I once made the serious mistake of believing I knew everything there was to know and no longer needed to study. Not only did I receive a failing grade, but I was forced to take a semester off and required to file an appeal before the Board before being allowed to resume my studies. What a humbling experience! Remember, we are never finished learning about ourselves or how the world works.

♦ **Leading you.** John Maxwell once said, "The hardest person to lead is yourself." True leaders figure out how to remain diligent, stay on track, be organized, stay focused, and lead themselves as well as others. If you weren't born with these traits, try volunteering for leadership positions in local churches or non-profit groups. *Simply make an offer to help.* The rewards that come back will be limitless!

Your intuition is ready to lead you. Are you ready to follow?

▦ *Meet the Contributor*

Sandra Harris holds a Masters degree in Physical Therapy from the University of Miami and a Bachelors degree in Athletic Training from San Diego State University. In addition to her active role in patient care she is owner and operator of Profits Marketing Group, a digital marketing agency that specializes in helping local medical and healthcare companies stand out from the competition using web video and targeted digital display ads.

Sandra's marketing strategies have boosted her clients' business leads by as much as 300 percent in as little as three months. Sandra is also a sought-after speaker and workshop presenter for SCORE San Diego, NAWBO, MGMA, Rotary, and other local business associations.

Leveraging her background in healthcare, Sandra recently started a new company to help primary care physicians and healthcare organizations improve patient care and increase revenue by streamlining the new Medicare Annual Wellness Visit (AWV). Sandra lives in San Diego, CA with her husband and two sons. You will often find her at the community center, cheering loudly while watching her husband Dan coach their two sons, Isaac and Alex.

Contact Sandra at http://AWVSuccessKit.com and http://ProfitsMarketingGroup.com.

FREEDOM STARTED
WITH A POTATO CHIP

DC Gilman (LBT #87)

WHAT IS ENTREPRENEURIAL success? Some would say it is pure luck. Some say it's pure hard work. And others say it's being in the right place at the right time with the right idea. All or part of each of these may be true. However, one of the greatest keys to entrepreneurial success is a lesson I learned as a teenager at the potato chip factory.

It was July in central Missouri. Most would say it was unbearable heat with stifling humidity. I guess I didn't know any better. I walked to work every day and was excited I had a job. The owner of the potato chip factory took a chance on this teenager and gave me a job for the summer. Bill, the owner, had introduced me to his system.

Success starts with a system. Every successful entrepreneur has a system for how they do things in their business, from the potato chip factory to McDonald's. Without a system a business is not a business. It is a sole proprietorship, a self-employed prison where everyone relies on the business owner to do the thinking for them. Sole is a lonely word, and even with employees you are by yourself.

If you cannot leave your business for at least a week and have it run without you, you have built a sole proprietorship, not a business. How do you get past this problem? Making time available to work *on* your business and not *in* your business is one of the greatest challenges for an entrepreneur, but it is the key to long-term success. It is the key driver in determining whether you have a business or a sole proprietorship.

Let me share with you the secret to creating effective systems. It's an easy one. It's called documentation. For every task you do, take a digital recorder, smartphone, or notepad — whatever method is easiest for you — and document every step you take when you are doing a task. Yes, it will take you a bit more time along the way, but this is the makings of your standard operating procedures manual — your business Bible, if you like — for the growth and development of your business. When you hire someone, your procedures manual provides a foundation for training. This is the first key to building a business and not a sole proprietorship.

The next step to entrepreneurial success is training. When I was the president of a national printing company, we were able to increase revenues from $15 million per year to over $21 million per year in less than five years. I didn't do it by myself. It took a team of people creating and improving procedures then properly training our employees to think for themselves. We implemented the effective training practices I learned early on in my corporate career and have embraced ever since. This involves putting your procedure in writing, demonstrating it, and then having the person do the task you are training.

All three steps are important. When you conduct training for new or existing personnel, actively involve the trainee in the process by having her read the process of doing the task, watch you doing the task, and then perform the task herself with you observing. This will accelerate the training, reduce your turnover, and (as we saw at the printing company) increase overall revenues as well because it allows you to scale your business effectively and efficiently.

People have various learning styles, and typically entrepreneurs will process new information using the style they are most comfortable with. However, learning specialists have proven that in order to retain a task, people need to have incorporated all three learning styles. That's what gives a piece of knowledge the "sticky" factor.

The next entrepreneurial success tip I learned was when the corporate ladder I was climbing ran out of rungs. I had spent over sixteen years with the printing company and had worked my way up from the entry level position. I worked my way into sales and became sales manager, then VP of Sales, then VP of Operations, and finally the last rung, president. That's the funny thing: I accepted the praise and compliments with a smile, but then someone said, "Now that you have achieved all of this, what's next?" It was that simple question that stumped me. I said, "I don't know." And that was the truth. I had run out of rungs on the corporate ladder. The next few months I spent a significant amount of time thinking about my next step and realized I needed to design my own ladder.

I needed a ladder that was horizontal and encompassed multiple streams of income, provided multiple options, and gave me the flexibility I desired. That's when I decided to immerse myself in the world of entrepreneurship and create my own destiny. That sounds ethereal, I know, but I took everything I learned in corporate America and decided to apply it to my own businesses.

The lesson I took away from this experience was that no one will care for your business as much as you do. That's just human nature. When you are in charge of your own company, it's your baby. If you want it to grow up and be strong, you have to take full responsibility for it. As you grow and diversify, remember that you will soon acquire a team. To get the people on that team to care like you do, you have to walk the talk, demonstrate, and be willing to do everything you ask of someone else.

Why did I jump out on my own? Why do so many people want to become entrepreneurs? One word: freedom. I determined I wanted freedom. However, that word means a lot of things to different people. For me, the freedom entrepreneurship brought was actually in the form of control — control of my destiny. If I wanted to get up and make something happen, I was the one who controlled my ability to do so. If I wanted to get up and work or not, that choice was mine and mine alone.

Most importantly, freedom also means control of your time. The fact that you are an entrepreneur, in and of itself, does not make you free. In fact, I know a lot of entrepreneurs who are slaves to their businesses. Let me clarify: slaves to their sole proprietorships. Being an entrepreneur doesn't automatically make you free; it just means your responsibilities have changed. If you are working for a "boss" your responsibility is to show up, do your job, and have a great attitude along the way. Being an entrepreneur means all of the responsibility is now yours. You are showing up for yourself and are also expected to "show up" mentally for everyone else on your team. The buck starts and stops with you. There is added pressure, but the rewards can far exceed the responsibility when you are focused on creating multiple passive income streams that allow you even more choice and freedom in the process.

Part of that process is yet another success secret, and that secret is goal setting. I know there are a lot of people who always preach about setting goals, and there is another camp of people who tell you to drop the goals, set a vision, and let the road pave itself in front of you. However, I believe goal setting actually supports your ability to have a strong vision, see clearly the direction you want to go, and take the next steps with confidence. And we all know the key to success in any business is taking action. Idle people remain idle.

I have learned what I believe is the greatest goal setting process that exists. It starts with creating your Directional Goals, then determining your Daily Action Steps, and finally identifying your To-Do List.

▨ DIRECTIONAL GOALS

These are the goals that you outline for yourself for the next 12 months. Then you work backwards and identify your goals for the next six months, then three months, then one month, then one week. This gives you the specifics for what you need to create the next step.

▨ DAILY ACTION STEPS

These are the things that you need to do on a consistent basis in order to achieve the long-term goals you identified. These can be things like:

- Read the Bible or your favorite book every day

- Read a chapter in a business improvement book each day

- Create mindful eating habits and journal your food intake

- Exercise or concentrate on a "movement" plan

- Mark x amount of items off the To-Do List

▓ To-Do List

The next thing is to create your to-do list for the day. This will list the specific items you need to complete each day in order to tick away at your goals. There are specific steps, projects, and items that need to be completed. Note those each day and mark them off. Then you will be one step closer to your goals.

This goal setting process supports the adage of how you eat an elephant: one bite at a time.

The last thing I want to share with you is that you have to believe and trust — even when others don't or won't. You have to. If you don't believe in yourself, in your product or service, then no one else will. It starts with an unwavering deep belief in yourself. This will allow you to move forward with faith, and it takes faith every day in this world. You may stumble and take a few hits, but it is much easier to bounce back when you are unwavering in your belief and faith. Build your system with checks and balances, so you can rely on others, too.

In summary, here are the keys to entrepreneurial success that I have experienced, tried, and proven effective:

- Create systems

- Document your procedures

- Define Freedom for you

  - Create passive income to give you choices and control

- Set goals

- Directional Goals

- Daily Action Steps

- To-Do Lists

  • Cultivate unwavering belief and faith

I would wish you luck, but where you are going you don't need luck. You are destined for greatness if you follow your heart, do what you love to do, and are passionate about everything you do in life. That has worked for me, and I now own over 80 rental properties, have become an author and international speaker, and have a Facebook gaming app that I am currently launching. It's not luck; just follow my success tips and I'll see you at the top!

■ *Meet the Contributor*

DC GILMAN is an author, speaker, entrepreneur, business owner, and a man with a mission — to teach financial literacy and entrepreneurial skills to young adults.

Born and raised in small-town Missouri, DC started working before he could drive. He moved from mowing lawns to serving as president of a printing company and owner of several businesses. Along the way, he realized he had followed the plan and work ethic his parents had instilled in him (the same work ethic their parents had shared), but he wanted something different, something more. He learned the advantage of working smarter (versus working harder) to achieve your goals. In 2011, after juggling his corporate life with an entrepreneurial dream, DC left his six-figure job to pursue his goal of creating his own business empire — and helping others to do the same.

Today, DC operates multiple businesses and manages several streams of revenue, from network marketing to real estate. His latest book, *Get Your Win On!* showcases the essential steps, attitude, and mindset for entrepreneurial success. DC is also co-author of *Marketing Miracles* with marketing guru Dan Kennedy. He has worked with and shared the stage with some of the most notable business strategists, marketing experts, and motivating personalities of our generation.

DC holds a BS in business administration from University of Central Missouri and is a graduate of the Dale Carnegie Course. He and his wife Kathy have two teenage daughters, Mikaela and Alana, who are building their own entrepreneurial empires.

Contact DC at www.DCGilman.com

Trust Your Gut — It Doesn't Lie

Deborah Johnson (LBT #49)

WHEN I GRADUATED from nursing school in Michigan in 1971, I wanted more than anything to travel. So for the next 15 years I did just that. What I owned I could put into my backpack. I made my way to California (didn't we all want to do that in the '70s?), living in Mendocino and San Francisco. Then it was on to Alaska, the South Pacific, New Zealand, and back to the US to live in Wisconsin and Washington. It was a wondrous exploration and discovery of the world.

In Washington I settled down to marriage and home ownership, and gave birth to my two sons. All during that time I knew I wanted to be in business for myself and joined just about every multi-level marketing program in existence, sometimes more than one at a time. My husband thought I was crazy or just money hungry, and couldn't understand why a regular job at the local hospital was unable to satisfy me. Inside I knew I wanted out of the job market, but I was not able to find my niche. Why, I often asked myself, was I so driven to step into the realm of self-employment? Why wasn't I happy with normal day-to-day work routines like everyone else? Was I going to continue trying every new scheme that was shown to me, feeling like a born loser, and never coming out ahead? At times I wondered if I was just going to drive myself nuts with this idea that I had to be self-employed.

Still, the compulsion was there and I couldn't deny it. I had to be self-employed. So I read the books I was told to read, and went to the rallies and conventions of yet another company and signed up with the next marketing idea.

What I didn't realize was that with every attempt to step into a new business I was learning skills I had not had before. I was learning how to motivate people and myself, and I was beginning my journey to find what it took to run a business, even when the "failure" was evident in my business bank account. I began to grow and change in ways I can only see clearly now.

Then one morning in 1995 I had a dream that I needed to move back to Michigan — the place I swore I would never return to. The dream left me with a sense of confidence and clarity I could not deny. The decision was so clear that I didn't even question the move. So within a few months my two boys, our cat, and a rat (yes, my kids had to have the rat move with us!) started on our month-long road trip back to Michigan where most of my family lived.

We bought a house near my family and began our life together in a new place. Within a few months my mother was diagnosed with a brain tumor. It became very clear to me why I was now in Michigan. I was able to be with my family during this time and assist in the care of my mother in a way that would not have been possible had I stayed in Washington. It was a time in my life when I felt very connected and knew I was in the right place at the right time. My mother passed within 18 months of her diagnosis, and I was there to grieve with and support my family.

Why have I added this to a story about business successes? To share with you my discovery that sometimes the universe seems to move us towards our dreams in a way that is "behind the scenes" and invisible at the beginning.

I began working at a home health agency during this time and, as was usual with me, I had a second job. I was now a single mom raising my two sons, and I always seemed to need more income. That need found me on the phone with my friend, asking her what she knew about the job market and how I could earn more income with my nursing degree.

She suggested I call her sister, who was working as a case manager with auto accident survivors. Curious as to what that job might entail, I followed up and soon found myself with a third job — case manager.

I didn't know anything about case management, and you may not either, so let me explain. A case manager is a licensed health care provider, in my case an RN, who oversees the medical care of those who are catastrophically injured. I was given the task of working with those individuals covered by Michigan's auto insurance who were injured in auto accidents. In Michigan, those catastrophically injured are allowed to partner with a case manager to ensure the care they receive is appropriate, reasonable, and necessary for their recovery from the injuries incurred in that accident.

Well, I had never had so much fun using my nursing skills. I was able to work with people who needed my expertise and view their progress as they went through their rehabilitation, which sometimes took many years. All my skills over the previous 40 years of nursing were finally being used. Not only that, I was able to schedule my services around my other jobs and my growing family. This role fit me to a T!

Then I received THE CALL. My supervisor called to say that I needed to drop my clients because she had a disagreement with the referral source. I argued that I couldn't just drop these people. They needed my services and I needed the income. Then she said the words that changed my life: "Then go into business for yourself." I remember exactly where I was at the time those words were spoken to me. It was one of those memorable moments we each have at major junctures in our lives.

So I did just that. I didn't know how, but I did know that this door was the one I had been waiting for. Careforward, LLC was born. I just thought, "Hell, I can do this business and I can find out what I don't know by finding others that do know. I can figure this out." The years of "failed" attempts at my multi-level marketing businesses, my studying and the compulsion to learn more about how I could be in business for myself, the untold monies spent on conferences and seminars — they all fell into place. Magic? I think not. I now see there was power in that undeniable, gut-wrenching determination to find the business that was right for me.

At that time, most case managers were affiliated with the insurance companies. I found that sometimes the case managers did not have the best interest of the client in mind when directing the care. So I decided my company (which was just me at the time) would obtain referrals from outside of the insurance companies. "Friends" told me this was *not* the way to run a case management business, and it would fail if I didn't take referrals directly from the insurance industry. But I was determined to do it my way.

When catastrophically injured patients and their families found out I would advocate for them with no hidden agenda, they began coming to me. Then care providers admired my approach and also began referring clients to me. Soon I had too many clients to manage by myself. I called my friends who were experienced RNs and let them know I was able to train them to set up their own businesses, instruct them on how to use their skills in case management, and would contract with them. By then, I had also hired a person to run the office, and she is still with me today. We have grown and learned together.

When I signed up to learn more at Loral Langemeier's Big Table #49, Careforward was at an annual gross of $300,000. Through Loral's instructions and the support of my colleagues and the Big Table alumni, we continued to grow.

I had no idea that over the next 10 years Careforward would expand to a business with over a million dollars annual gross income and more than 16 self-employed RN case managers contracting with Careforward to deliver services in Michigan, and now in Florida as well. And we are still growing through times in which many other businesses are failing. Why? Because it is my passion. I'm willing to learn what I don't know and partner with others who are in alignment with my goals.

So if you have that nagging feeling in your gut, if you've tried many times to find your niche, my message to you is: "Don't give up." There is a reason, maybe beyond what you can now see, and a purpose that lies perhaps just around the next corner. The world needs your talents now.

It is our small businesses that will move our economy, both personally and nationally, to the next level. Find your passion and believe your gut when it says, "I was not born to be an employee. There is more out there for me and I will find it."

I wish you Joy and Love on your journey.

■ Meet the Contributor

DEBORAH JOHNSON, RN, is the owner and founder of Careforward, LLC, an auto injury case management firm based in Southfield, Michigan. She is a Certified Case Manager and a Certified Brain Injury Specialist. She is a former president of the Case Management Society of America, Detroit Chapter. She has won several awards, among them the 2010 Top 10 Women Business Owners Award presented by the National Association of Women Business Owners; the 2010 and the 2011 National Award for Independent Case Management presented by Case In Point; and the 2010 award for Education/Public Awareness of Brain Injury presented by the Michigan Brain Injury Association. She now has case managers throughout Michigan and Florida.

Her second business is CareInsight, LLC (www.careinsight.net). As a Certified Dementia Practitioner, Deborah provides geriatric, pediatric, and disability care management services.

She is the founder and president of the Board of the Careforward Foundation, Inc., a 501(c)(3) nonprofit organization (www.carnivalofcare. org), whose vision is "We envision a day when all people impacted by catastrophic injury are celebrated, cherished, embraced, and honored."

You can contact Deborah at www.careforward.com or djohnson@ careforward.com.

RESILIENCY: DISCOVER OPPORTUNITY WITHIN ADVERSITY

Fred Smith (LBT #91)

"A smooth sea never made a skilled sailor."
— English Proverb

WHEN I WAS FIVE YEARS OLD, I knew there was something wrong with the way the outside world appeared before my eyes. I lived in Chester, Pennsylvania, an impoverished industrial inner-city area just outside of Philadelphia, where I could see the hard racial lines of city neighborhoods that are still segregated to this day.

I was amazed at how dirty and dingy the city was, and how the sky waxed gray due to pollution painting the atmosphere. Oil refineries, steel mills, and industrial parks dotted and scorched the atmosphere with gray fallout clouds all around me, spiraling and crawling upwards through tall chimneys. The air always had a certain smell — a general combination of smelt and oil, depending upon which grim reaper disciple was competing for my nose that day or whatever industry felt compelled to go into overdrive and produce more.

The concrete jungle, combined with poverty, drugs, and violence, was not designed to nurture my soul.

The years went by and one summer day, after a major rainstorm had just passed, something magical happened to me. I was walking by the freeway not too far from where I lived. On my left, cars loudly buzzed and whizzed by. I could hear the water filling the wheel wells and cars hitting puddles, scrambling for traction. On my right side, 50 feet above the interstate from where I was standing, was an athletic field with acres of green grass for track, football, soccer, and related sports. And as I was contemplating the meaning of life, particularly my life, I cannot explain how everything came together at that particular moment — except to say, it was divine.

As I looked up into the sky, I believe I watched a miracle unfold. The sky was changing right in front of my eyes. The wind was pushing the muck from east to west. On the right side of me was a wonderfully clear blue sky, with fluffy white cumulus clouds starting to reveal themselves. The sun started penetrating the gray and rancid sky to the left of me, and I could feel its warmth penetrate my right shoulder and eventually envelop me. The light began beaming through the darkness of the recent storm. Eventually, the heat and humidity from the moist air and sudden illumination became almost unbearable, as if someone had thrown me into a swamp.

Within what seemed like minutes to me the whole sky became clear, with just the humidity and rain puddles left to bear. I just stood there in awe, watching this beautiful process manifest and unfold right in front of my young eyes. That day, I discovered duality, the key that unlocked my drive, motivation, determination, and resiliency to make things happen in my life.

That day has stuck with me forever, and I've followed the one simple principle I learned: to elevate myself against superior odds that were stacked against me.

I realized resiliency in particular was important to achieve greater success in life, because I had to learn how to travel the road of dichotomy. Those days spent living through the trials and tribulations of my life created a permanent foundation for my understanding of the trials of the human condition. Short of being homeless (which I was a few times),

I knew I couldn't get any lower in life. But those experiences gave me the fuel I needed to convert stress into motivation and challenge myself to look within to discover the answers I needed to create change in my life and become an alchemist.

My humble experience of developing resiliency pales in comparison to someone who has experienced totalitarian conditions or a holocaust. Nevertheless, my experience has given me a baseline of which I am aware. I believe everyone has one, but the question is, are they aware enough to realize where the "You are Here" position is on the Map of Life?

Adversity will develop and challenge your mindset and courage, and influence your commitment to what you'd like to achieve in life. Overcoming adversity involves discovering the path, walking the path, and deciding to live the path you've created for yourself. I've discovered that resiliency is the bridge on the journey between points A and B that tests your mettle and answers that nagging question: "Is this what I really want?"

Ultimately, resiliency is the fuel I need to evolve to the next level in my life and to grow bigger than my challenges and obstacles. It's the thing that allows me to develop a constant and never-ending improvement mindset to stay consistent and true to what I want to manifest in my life. The road to success is filled with failure. The key is to fail forward, not backwards. How is this done? By recognizing the only constant in this equation is change. Any amount of change can be overcome by embracing resiliency and using it to add more fuel to our will to succeed.

When I was developing my resiliency muscles, I realized there were several steps involved. The first one was letting go of my limiting beliefs and developing the skill of getting out of my own way. I then started to see self-defeating patterns that sabotaged my confidence and belief that I could get from point A to B. The biggest skill I developed was patience. Resiliency requires a lot of control, relinquishment, endurance, and especially patience while things are evolving. But I realized that I was developing and evolving into more; that my goals, dreams, and aspirations were not events but actual processes — sometimes processes within processes. I understood they would manifest in their time, not mine. That was a huge step for me. Resiliency is the ability to hang in there while things are brewing and cooking themselves up.

We are unfortunately living in the days where microwave popcorn is now too slow. I remember the days when I had a gas stove and a manual popcorn popper and popping it was a true event and process. If you start developing your resiliency muscles every day after reading this, within 30 days you'll start developing your groove. You'll realize that every action you take may require micro actions before the macro outcome, but because you've chosen to be resilient and steadfast in your actions, you'll see patterns emerging. Then you'll be able to see if they serve you or hurt you, and you can adjust accordingly, based on your definition of success and where you are on the Map of Life.

I see several self-imposed roadblocks that prevent people from getting started with developing this critical muscle. Most people think their life is in too much chaos or they are unorganized or simply locked in analysis paralysis. But these are the exact reasons why you should begin. These factors are knocking on your door, some of them banging on it.

You've already proven you're resilient. Unfortunately you've been resilient in not doing anything about your situation and gotten stuck in some way. A powerful strategy that's worked for me has been to focus my energy by simplifying everything first. Then I develop one stable point in the chaos, confusion, etc., and just handle that one thing to completion. Then two things, followed by four, etc. The next thing you know, success becomes a geometrical progression, and the cycle starts all over again — this time with challenges bigger than the last time. It's an evolution, not a destination.

Resiliency is the lubricant in the wheel of life, the flow needed to keep you on the go. Just don't give up — that's the secret. Remember the dichotomy. If there's an up, there's a down, and navigating the rough seas to your next destination IS the journey of resiliency itself.

Don't give up. Albert Einstein says it best: "In the middle of difficulty lies opportunity."

The first physical action step I challenge you to do is map out everything you want. Ask yourself the following questions:

1. "What specifically do I want?"

2. "Where am I now?"

3. "How will I know when I have what I want?"

4. "What will I see, hear, and feel when I have it?"

5. "What will this outcome get for me or allow me to do?"

6. "What do I have now, and what do I need in order to get to my outcome?"

Take this template of questions. Make uninterrupted time for yourself to deeply contemplate these questions and be as specific as possible in your answers. Once you've made the decision to say, "I'm mad as hell, and I'm not going to take it anymore!" the motivation to take massive and immediate action will appear. You'll quickly discover your thoughts lead to feelings, then to actions, and ultimately to results. In between the actions and results lies resiliency. Discover your opportunity within adversity, and allow the sun to shine on your shoulder as it did on mine.

■ Meet the Contributor

Fred Smith is an award-winning intrapreneur, thought leader, investor, and educator who specializes in monetizing business opportunities at a global scale. A highly sought-after marketing and sales trainer and performance coach, he has successfully assisted scores of people ranging from individuals boot-strapping their small businesses, to sales professionals and executives looking to get to the next level, and even multi-national corporations already dominating their niches. Change the bottom-line marketing and sales results in your business: contact Fred at www.TheGameExposed.com."

Marilyn Monroe, Magic, & Marketing

Timothy Noonan (LBT #79)

WHAT DO MARILYN MONROE, a magician, and internet marketing have in common (besides all starting with the letter "M")?

I'll tell you that in a moment, but first I want to tell you a little about myself. I am known as the "Biz Launch Guy," because I help aspiring entrepreneurs quickly and easily build a brand, create a product line, and launch their business. I am also a professional magician, author, and internet marketer. I have a passion for helping people quickly and easily turn their knowledge into a successful business.

Before I continue with the story, I would like to ask a favor. Please take a moment to ponder one word, focusing on what you feel it means to you: Success.

Like it or not, we all strive for success in some way. To many people, it seems to be equated with acquiring money, a new home or car, wardrobe, or building a business.

For me, success is all about pursuing my passions while helping people create successful business endeavors.

I grew up a bit different than the average kid. My parents never had a mainstream job; they were unique for their time. My father was a professional actor and entrepreneur. You might have seen him in movies like

"A Star is Born" with Judy Garland, or "Gentlemen Prefer Blondes" with Marilyn Monroe. (He is easy to spot; he marries Marilyn in the movie.) My mother was a professional dancer. So when I was growing up as a kid in Los Angeles, there was a constant parade of movie stars in and out of our house. We lived well in a large house and with few worries.

I am the youngest of four children. I have an older brother and two older sisters. We had a pretty easy life — until I was about six years old. My father decided that he was tired of being a slave to the movie studio, and when his contract was up with Warner Brothers, he made the radical decision to open his own movie studio, Harlequin International Pictures. He borrowed $300,000 from investors, rented land, and began building. I have vague memories of listening to him discussing his plans for the family with my mother, so excited to be following his dream. I remember him constantly saying, "I am following my heart! I am following my passion! Marilyn made it, so can I!" to justify his choices.

Then, a few weeks into his project, disaster struck.

We were sitting on the sofa, watching TV. Suddenly, my father went into convulsions and fell on the floor. My mother and I struggled to get him back on the sofa, and then she called an ambulance and he was rushed to the hospital.

He was diagnosed with a malignant brain tumor. He was 45 years old — with no insurance, four kids, and just a few months left to live.

I remember visiting him in the hospital, listening to him talk about his plans for when he got better, the movie ideas he had, and plans for the family. Not knowing the full extent of the problem, I was convinced he would be home soon. I was wrong. A few months later, my father passed away. I was six years old.

As a teenager, I was fascinated with magic. I had a friend who knew a few tricks, and so I convinced him to teach me. Eventually, I decided to become a full-time magician. After a few years of hard work and low income, I began to have some success. I kept at it. Eventually, I had my own show at the MGM Grand in Las Vegas. I then built an internet business, as technology has always been a passion of mine as well.

I figured that even though I was successful as a performer, I should have a backup business model in place to supplement my income, "just in case." Eventually, I found some success online as well. I eventually started over 20 web-based businesses.

During my life journey, I observed something about myself, and cultivated this knowledge. I felt (and still feel) that I have a unique gift: I am not only able to become successful at my own endeavors, but I have the ability to observe my process, streamline it, and — most importantly — articulate and replicate my process.

For example, I have the ability to see where others get stuck in the online business model, and I can find the most effective way to break through and help them achieve success. So I began helping others become successful through internet marketing.

All of this knowledge I attribute to the experience I went through as a child. It was like a flower slowly blooming, each experience built upon the lessons of the last, until a certain level of wisdom and clarity was achieved.

Here are the seven most important success lessons I have learned thus far. Some apply to business, some apply to life, and some apply to both. I want to share them with you:

▨ TIME IS SHORT

Whatever you are doing, realize that time is passing. Let go of the things that do not serve a higher purpose in your life. Focus on what matters to you and your loved ones. In business, plan your work and work your plan. In life, live fully and communicate clearly. Angels fly because they are light.

▨ EFFICIENCY IS KEY

When I wanted to have a show in Vegas, I found the top booking agent who could make it happen. When I wanted to learn internet marketing, I asked around for the best, and found a mentor. Mentors will save you time and effort by fast tracking the process. Find the right mentor and work with him or her. There might be more than one, depending upon the business.

■ ONE CHOICE IS NO CHOICE

Having only one process can be a disaster to your business. What if the process or business model becomes outdated or useless? Having a backup process or model is essential. Also, have redundant teams in place. For my video projects, I use one editor, but I found someone who can do what he does as well, in case he is not available when I need him. Have a backup system, process, and team in place BEFORE you need them.

■ BUSINESS AND LIFE ARE DYNAMIC – TRUST BUT VERIFY

Nothing is static; everything expands, contracts, and changes. Everything IS process. There is a time for business and a time for family. Learn the distinction. Be sensitive to the moment, and respond accordingly.

Having a mentor who understands that there might be more than one way to run a business is important, because anyone who becomes stuck in one way of doing things ignores the basic rule of change. Find a mentor who is open to having you learn from different sources. Make sure they can explain the "why" of what they teach, and weigh their reasoning with your own judgment.

■ KEEP IT SIMPLE

All business systems need to be (fairly) simple. Create a map of your business, and find the most effective, simple way to get from point A to point B. Streamline, use the latest tools, keep updating your processes and systems, and be effective. Do not confuse motion with action.

■ LEARN TO RESPOND, NOT TO REACT

Most people today live in a very reactive mental state. If you don't believe me, just read some YouTube comments on any popular video! Take the time to respond, rather than react. This means being able to remove emotion from the process, understand what you are experiencing, and weigh and process it before answering or taking action.

Develop a balance between logic and emotion. The whole point of conversation is to understand where the other person is coming from, how they see the situation, and why. Listen, don't just "hear."

▨ MAKE THE WORLD BETTER BY GIVING BACK

Take the time to give back to the world. You can do that with a helping hand, a kind word, or being there in silence when you are needed. Too many people only offer to help because they have an agenda. There is great wisdom in putting down any agenda, and simply helping others with no thought of reward or gain. The Chinese character for "Give" and "Gain" is the same.

▨ FINAL THOUGHTS

I believe our legacy to this world is how we keep our mind, live our life, and do things. Be the example of what you want to manifest. Spend time with loved ones, put down business when necessary, and live your life fully.

I would like to end with a quote by Reinhold Niebuhr, a Protestant theologian:

"Nothing worth doing is completed in our lifetime, therefore we must be saved by hope. Nothing true or beautiful or good makes complete sense in any immediate context of history, therefore we must be saved by faith. Nothing we do, however virtuous, can be accomplished alone. Therefore we must be saved by love."

To your success,
Timothy Noonan
Las Vegas, NV

Meet the Contributor

KNOWN AS "THE BIZ LAUNCH GUY", Timothy Noonan is a master of helping people turn their passion into revenue. An inspiring coach & product creation expert, he has shared the stage with some of the top thought leaders and Fortune 100 executives of our time. Timothy has spent the last 10 years developing unique resources to help entrepreneurs quickly build a brand, create a product line, and launch a business. Download his free special report entitled: "Marketing Your Expertise The Smart Way" at his website. You can contact Timothy today at www.BizLaunchGuy.com

You Are Never Too Old to Follow Your Dreams

Shirley Vaughn, DMin (LBT #87)

I HAVE HAD A LOVE for the Bible ever since I can remember. My mother often read it to me when I was a young child. I received my first Bible in the third grade. I have been reading it ever since. It has been the touchstone for my life.

When I finished high school, I did not want to work full-time. Instead, I worked part-time and went to a junior college in Los Angeles. It was during this time that I had an encounter with Jesus and gave my heart and life to the Lord.

After junior college, I continued my education at U.C.L.A., where I majored in home economics and minored in finance. This proved to be great preparation for marriage because the classes that I took taught me the basics on how to run a home and balance a checkbook. After I had completed two and a half years of college study, I worked at Richfield Oil's credit department for a period of ten years. During this time, I continued to take night classes at college.

The Lord then led me to go to San Diego State College, where I finished my education and graduated with a BA in home economics and finance. During this time I was looking for my lifetime roommate. I figured that if I did not find my husband there I would go to Talbot Seminary.

I met Gregory Vaughn in San Diego. We got married quietly in October 1970, then we had a church wedding in December. During the majority of our forty-plus years of marriage, I have been disabled. In spite of my disability, I continued attending classes at a nearby junior college in Fresno, California.

After a period of time I found that a charismatic church I was attending on Sunday evening had a Bible school connected with it. I attended the Bible school for several years, taking one class at a time. Just before completing my course of study with the Bible school, it became accredited and I graduated with a BA in Bible. I then attended Friends International Christian University for a period of about twenty years. My emphasis of study was the Old Testament with a Messianic Jewish slant. When I was preparing for my master's degree in Bible, the Lord gave me the vision for my thesis: "God's March to the New Jerusalem." The purpose of the thesis was to show how God, through the ages, meets man in various places of worship.

I tried for about fifteen years to finish my master's thesis, but the time was not right. Moreover, I did not have the needed finances or a qualified person to take on such a tremendous project of putting this information on the computer. Nevertheless, during those years I continued to collect valuable information in support of my thesis, and I filed this material for future use. I asked the Lord to provide for my financial needs as well as someone to help with the work around the house. I also asked for someone who was very competent with computers.

My prayers were answered. About five years ago, MK Ferguson offered to help me with this massive project, because she believed in what the book could do for the Christian community as much as I did. As a result, work on my thesis officially resumed. My advisor told me that I had eighteen months to complete it. I was able to get a one month extension, as it took a total of nineteen months to complete the 623 page thesis.

After my advisor received the disk with the master's thesis on it, he called me into his office and said, "I am sorry, this is not a master's thesis." He paused. Then he said, "It is a doctorate because of all the material that has been covered in the book." And that is how, in October 2008, I received a doctor of ministry degree in religious studies.

The thesis is currently being put into book format by Xulon Press, which will also be responsible for publishing it.

God's March to the New Jerusalem is an easy-to-read reference book. It is arranged in chronological order and provides readers with a better understanding of the Bible and current events. As a result of studying this book, you will understand the Bible in a matter of weeks of study instead of years.

Some of the challenges I encountered along this journey tested my resolve to complete this project. For example, I experienced some website problems that are being resolved by Web page design specialists within Loral Langemeier's Live Out Loud community. I appreciate the team of coaches and fellow entrepreneurs found within this community, because it fosters success in so many business areas, including book publishing, launching a business, or generating new leads through effective marketing.

I never gave up on the idea of publishing *God's March to the New Jerusalem*, even though there were many challenges I faced with the production and distribution of the book. I knew that this was what I was supposed to do. God put this dream in me so that it might be fulfilled.

My advice to you, the reader: Never give up on *your* dream regardless of your situation. We all have a part to play on the stage of life. Fulfill the dream that is within you.

■ *Meet the Contributor*

SHIRLEY VAUGHN married her husband in 1979 and later graduated from Victory Christian Bible School in 1989 with a BA in Bible studies. She received a doctorate of ministry in religious studies from Friends International Christian University in October 2008. The topic and compilation of her doctoral thesis was inspired by God. This eventually led to the development of the book *God's March to the New Jerusalem.*

Contact Shirley at www.godsmarch.com.

Living Beyond Boundaries: How to Exceed Your Own Expectations

Claudia Sophia Hernandez (LBT #90)

All who have accomplished great things have had a great aim, have fixed their gaze on a goal which was high, one which sometimes seemed impossible.
— Orison Swett Maden

THE PATH TO SUCCESS is unique for every one of us. Each time we face an obstacle or challenge, we are given the opportunity to accept limitations or push past them to achieve our individual goals. My own story isn't always an easy one to tell, but I like to focus on the ultimate triumph: the end result. As the President and CEO of EXIT Realty, Financial Advisor at World Financial Group, and Founder/President of Cloud 9 Enterprises, LLC, I strive to honor my professional responsibilities to my clients and colleagues, and to inspire others through an unwavering vision of success. Many people searching for their own victories seek specific steps to help them accomplish their goals. Those steps do exist, but you've got to be prepared. You must be ready to embark upon your own distinct journey, and you must have a clear idea of what your final destination will be.

Early in life, my path was one that coursed through two countries, two languages, and two cultures. My parents, natives of Mexico, raised six children in the United States. While my siblings and I were geographically American, we were brought up in an environment that celebrated and valued our parents' traditions as well. Growing up, it was tough at times to figure out who I was or what I was supposed to be. But rather than limit myself to a predetermined template, I realized I had the opportunity to create the life I wanted for myself. I was driven, hardworking and had an entrepreneurial spirit that was ripe for development. I knew those character traits would get me somewhere in life. As a teenager, I just wasn't sure where I wanted to go.

When I was in high school, my potential caught the eye of a local business owner. She hired me to be her personal assistant, and I jumped at the chance to absorb as much knowledge from her as possible. I was determined to make something of myself, to realize the American dream. At 19 years old, I negotiated an arrangement to purchase the company from her. This was huge; at an age when most of my peers were still fantasizing about their first steps to financial independence and their professional futures, I was hitting the ground running. Within a few years of acquiring the business, I became the primary breadwinner for my family. Looking back, I credit my early success to a certain amount of innocence. You see, I never imagined this was something that was beyond my abilities. There were no obvious limits, so I never doubted my capacity to accomplish my goals. Without boundaries, I didn't need to worry I wouldn't fit the mold.

Every path, though, has its bumps. I made my share of mistakes, partly because I didn't have an understanding of the parameters that, in fact, would keep me on course. With an outgoing personality and a tremendous sense of enthusiasm, I figured I had what was necessary to meet any challenge head-on. That didn't always work! I discovered formal training would allow me to capitalize on my strengths while identifying areas for improvement. I also needed to acquire basic information that extended beyond my scope of knowledge. Formal education will broaden your horizons, and there's an amazing wealth of experiential wisdom to be gained from a mentor or trainer. If you want to build a team, you've got to establish yourself as a leader first. Investing in yourself will pay significant dividends throughout the course of your career.

For me, getting started on the road to success was the easy part. Although I had no worries about the potential for failure, I've seen many amazing individuals who find themselves stalled at that starting point. They allow those boundaries to permeate their thoughts, and they succumb to the concerns that they aren't cut from the right cloth. My aim is to dispel that notion, to remind people we are all constantly evolving and have the potential to define and redefine ourselves. What's stopping *you*, right now, from breaking convention and establishing your own template for success?

Like many successful business professionals, I have been incredibly inspired by the insight of Zig Ziglar. He said, "If you can dream it, then you can achieve it. You will get all you want in life if you help other people get what they want." That's huge! Think about it — with a vision and a burning desire to succeed, you have all the potential in the world to reach your goals. So don't limit yourself. Are you young? Penniless? Inexperienced? Fantastic! You stand poised to become as successful as you please. That's because conditions like these give you an advantage that can't be matched by any amount of education, upbringing, or money you might think you need to begin your journey. Consider this: according to Felix Dennis, author of *How to be Rich*, an overwhelming majority of the fortunes acquired by entrepreneurs came to individuals who invested so much of themselves because they had nothing to lose.

Once you have accepted the idea you needn't be limited by convention, you'll be ready to explore the abundance of opportunities around you. This is where boundaries will become your allies. To chart a course to success, you must have an idea of what that success looks like. Whether your definition of the end result is incredibly specific or somewhat unrefined, you will greatly increase your odds of accomplishing your goals when you keep them at the forefront of your thoughts, guiding your actions.

Remember also that success may come to you in many forms. For example, when I purchased the employment agency I had no idea I'd one day be the owner of a thriving real estate brokerage. What I did know — what I saw very clearly — was that I was going to be successful and that I'd lead others to success as well.

In my own entrepreneurial journey, there were five critical components to success. These, I believe, are the stepping stones on any professional path and I am excited to share them with you.

1. Mindset

2. Desire

3. Leadership

4. Persistence

5. Passion

The right **mindset** will establish a foundation upon which your success will be built. Having it is half the battle; it can carry you through tough times or help you stay focused in the face of adversity. I told myself early on failure wasn't an option. It was sink or swim, and I never had any intentions of hitting the bottom. My driving philosophy is that nothing is impossible and while the difficult takes time, the impossible just takes a little longer. Sounds easier said than done? We all face doubts, but I encourage you to take charge of your mindset. Don't let fear of failure run rampant through your thoughts. Harness it, acknowledge it, and put it aside. Failure doesn't need to trip you up on your path to success.

Your journey may become arduous at times, but a burning **desire** to achieve your goals will help you remain focused and driven. Are you truly committed to your goal? You've got to be willing to do what it takes to arrive at your final destination. If you really want something, you've got to keep it in your sights even when challenges pose a significant distraction. Ask yourself, *What price am I willing to pay to reach my objective?* If you know there's nothing you wouldn't do to make it happen, then you've got the desire necessary to get you through the hard times. If you don't, then you might want to reevaluate your goals and determine where your passions truly lie.

A strong sense of **leadership** is one of the elements of an entrepreneur's success that is frequently overlooked. Vision, creativity, and drive are imperative, but you aren't alone on your journey. The day we decide to become true leaders, we broaden our paths to include our employees. Our responsibilities, then, include the inspiration and nurturing of others. Imagine your path, lined with young trees that each contribute to a rewarding and memorable journey. Your employees are like those trees, and your job is to ensure that every one has the opportunity to find a perfect fit and grow along the route. And that route, incidentally, may change. A great leader looks at the materials at hand and adapts accordingly. Allow your path to diverge, and you may discover a destination you never imagined.

Persistence and **passion** are complimentary attributes for the successful entrepreneur. When you love what you do, when you are truly invested in your goals, you'll never ever take "no" for an answer. And believe me, there will be "no's." But I can attest to the fact that it's all worth the effort. You have what it takes to call the shots, inspire others, and create your dream lifestyle.

You are the master of your fate, the only one who can truly define who you are and what you can accomplish. Are you limiting yourself with worries, fears, or concerns? Your path has limitless possibilities! All you need to do is get started. Take the first step and you'll find that you're that much closer to your destination on your journey to success.

◼ *Meet the Contributor*

CLAUDIA SOPHIA HERNANDEZ is Founder, Co-Founder, and President of several successful businesses. She stands for leadership, inspiration, and the desire to make a difference for others — whether in business or in personal life. Claudia holds a BA in Business Administration (with emphasis on Leadership) from Chapman University and also an Interior Designers Institute Certificate.

Her next chapter in life is becoming an author and inspirational speaker to inspire and empower others to be their best self.

Throughout her education and career Claudia has been honored with many awards, including recognition in Cambridge Who's Who and receipt of the Orange County 5 Star Award for Professional REALTORS®. She is also a member of the National Association of Hispanic Real Estate Professionals (NAHREP), REOMac, and the former CFO of the Orange County Association of Real Estate Brokers (OCAREB). Contact Claudia at www.myreoproperties.com.

What Becoming a Mother Can Teach You About Business

Irma Hypes (LBT #83)

As a teen, I wasn't interested in infants or children and never had a babysitting job. As a young adult, when I encountered a new mom, her arms outstretched to hand me her baby, I would accept the infant with reservation. I held him like a hot casserole: not too close, but I wouldn't drop him either. Truth be told, I never had a maternal bone in my body — until I had my own child, which effectively put my 15-year career on hold.

Prior to becoming a mother, I had been a W-2 employee. My job description had already been defined. My role was marketing-specific. I did my work and got paid. I participated in board of directors meetings, managed my department's budget, hired my staff, and helped in other areas of my employers' business.

But no matter how determined and excited I was to start a family or a business, all the research, books, and advice in the world never *really* prepared me for the parental and entrepreneurial journey I embarked on. It has been an experience I could never have imagined, until now.

▪ THE BIRTH OF MY MARKETING COMPANY™

As many new mothers will tell you, there is a sense of guilt (among many other emotions) when you have to leave your child to complete even the simplest of tasks. Whether it's going back to work, on a date, or for a workout, leaving your precious one can be difficult. No one cares for him the same way you do — not even dad or grandma! And if your child shows separation anxiety during the transition, that bolt of guilt strikes you even stronger!

I returned to work when my first child was just three months old. I waited five months before returning to work after having my second child, but I worked that job for only two more months before being blessed with the opportunity to be a stay-at-home-mom (SAHM). Who better to raise and care for my children than me?

During the subsequent 18 months of caring for my children, I experienced a sense of discomfort I never could've imagined. Not only did I have to care for them, but I also had to keep house, walk the dog, make meals, do laundry, and grocery shop. We couldn't afford a nanny or housekeeper on one salary, so I had to learn how to do all of it.

I started My Marketing Company™ when my children were 2 and 3 years old. A business-owner friend asked if I could help her with marketing. The project didn't require more than a few hours of work per week and that work sparked something from within that I hadn't felt in a while. I loved my children, but I also felt a need for another kind of fulfillment. I felt the need to go back to work!

▪ GET ME OUT OF HERE!

As a SAHM my schedule revolved around the kids, their feeding, nap schedules, and activities. For example, I would grocery shop on a Tuesday morning; go for workouts on Friday at 3p.m.; and do a load of laundry in the middle of the day; all times being chosen to accommodate the schedules of the children. And unlike any other job, I took a nap when the kids napped. I had routines, but if they didn't happen on a certain day, it just meant everything got pushed back a day.

Being a work-at-home-mom (WAHM) was a totally different ball game. It required a proactive attitude and a business mindset; both had lain dormant during my time as a SAHM. Initially, I would sit down to work and find myself looking around the house. All of a sudden, laundry wasn't such a chore. The cold calls were. Doing the dishes was relaxing and vacuuming was calming. Leaving voicemails and hearing "No" was not!

Housework became an excuse to avoid progress. It was stopping me from doing the things I needed to do to get my business off the ground. The bottom line: working from home proved to be a huge distraction for me. I had to get out!

The alternatives to working from home presented their own challenges. Cafés were noisy and not conducive to making phone calls. Libraries were quiet, but were not conducive to making phone calls either. I was just starting out and couldn't afford or justify a private office.

Then another business owner-friend of mine mentioned I could use a desk at her office a couple times a week. Perfect! Here's the beautiful thing about *going* to work: you're not home for the dust bunnies to taunt you.

Alas, after a few months, my W-2 persona surfaced. I found myself avoiding my cold calls and lead-generation activities. Instead, I was socializing and having inane water cooler conversations. Then I read an article about the characteristics common to successful entrepreneurs and realized I wasn't *acting* like one. Even with departmental responsibilities in my W-2 job, I didn't have a clue how to be an entrepreneur. Knowing that I wanted something bigger from my company, I sought Loral Langemeier and the Live Out Loud community for coaching.

■ HOW BUSINESSES AND BABIES ARE THE SAME

Since attending the Big Table, I've learned a lot about entrepreneurship. The biggest take-away for me was to GET HELP! I did it as a new mother, so why didn't it dawn on me sooner that I needed it as a new business owner?

The Live Out Loud coaches and the Master Mind groups from my year at Big Table have been a contributing factor to the growth of my business. I learned that successful business owners have a team, and now I have one, too: my accountant, lawyer, and Master Mind group. They hold me responsible for what I say I am going to do and challenge me beyond my level of comfort.

From my Master Mind group, I learned it didn't matter if I worked from home or at an office. I just needed to set boundaries! They reminded me that if I were a W-2 employee, the housework would have to wait until I got home. Once I gave myself permission to ignore the house during "business hours," I felt liberated.

I work from home now. It doesn't mean that there aren't still days that I sweep to avoid bookkeeping. However, when I slip I just rearrange my schedule so that it works for me.

And remember that feeling of (pick an emotion) when I left my kids with a caregiver? I didn't become a parent so I could tell my children to do it my way the rest of their lives (although that would be great, wouldn't it?). I know it's healthy for my children to learn how to manage without me and that my role is to prepare them to be independent, self-fulfilled, contributing members of society.

The same goes for my business. You see, I'm at the point where I have to leave my newest baby (the business) in the hands of trusted staff. As the founder, my passion is at the core of the business and I am molding and shaping the brand. However, I don't plan to be the keystone of the day-to-day operations. Because my company characteristics and values will resonate with my employees, I *am* serving each and every client, even if I'm not as involved with every one of them.

▥ *Meet the Contributor*

IRMA HYPES is a professional marketing consultant with more than 18 years of industry experience spanning a variety of nationally-recognized brands. In 2010, Irma founded My Marketing Company™, offering strategic marketing and planning solutions to entrepreneurs and small business owners. She extends her marketing expertise to her community through the San Francisco Small Business Development Center and volunteers with Taproot Foundation. Irma received her bachelor of science in marketing degree from the University of Illinois at Chicago. To receive a free 30-minute marketing assessment, email her at irma@mymarketingcompanysf.com.

If Speaking Were Music,
It Would Be a Score

Pam Whitman, MA (LBT #88)

Music is love. Love is passion. Passion drives Beingness.
The Score orchestrates the Passion and Love,
creating a Story to convey the Message.

THIRTEEN YEARS AGO I found myself without a score. My life as I'd known it and expected it to play out was ending. I was very frightened, hurt, angry, and feeling alone in the throes of divorce. It felt as if I had contracted a disease making me an outcast from society. I cried every day and sang my heart out with all the songs of lost love I knew. Lyrics gave expression to my sadness and loss — melodic and rhythmic. What was I going to do, how would I survive, who would love me now, how would I make a new life, where would I find help? What was my score now?

Those initial days were torture. I had to take them one step at a time. Creating my new "normal" had me reaching inside to find what I loved. What filled my heart and awakened my desire to continue growing and exploring my gifts? I discovered my love of music and performing had been suppressed for years. I began singing and playing the piano again. Lyrics gave expression to my sadness and loss, and their melody and rhythm became a necessary component to my self-reinvention.

■ WHY WE ALL CAN CONNECT TO MUSIC

I remembered two musical scores that have always inspired me and speak to my spirit. Edward MacDowell's *To a Wild Rose* and Ferde Grofé's *Grand Canyon Suite* bring to life vivid images and the message that life is beautiful and definitely worth playing in. The themes of quiet and some dissonance lead to supporting harmonies, giving a sense of rebirth from emotional pain to feeling more whole and connected to the world.

Additionally, I joined a speaking program where I didn't have to speak. I was totally blown away and relieved by that concept. I didn't have to create something profound, didn't have to be polished, and didn't have to project. I just showed up, week after week. I was fascinated with the program. I would imagine I was on stage, the curtains opened and then I was connecting with each individual silently, just me as I am every day. It was like holding my babies, gazing on them with love and deep appreciation. I was practicing being present, being connected and grounded without saying a word. I learned that I had a right to the stage, and that my body and mind could be comfortable and actually revel in being in front of a group. It was astounding to receive appreciation (applause) for just being me and learn that people are interested and eager to accept me just as I am.

This wasn't as simple as it may sound. Every time I repeated this silent movement, I discovered more about who I had become in my body, thinking, and beliefs. I discovered I was very self-critical and judgmental; I was hiding. I made a commitment to watch the videos that came with the workshop, doing my best to listen and observe in a neutral and appreciative way. Amazingly, this gave me an appreciation for who I am and the expertise I possess.

In creating my presentations the challenge was that I was the author — it was my story and my dream, my passion. As I practiced I began to see how to score my presentations with a beginning, middle, and end — all in just three minutes. I discovered the secret within the score is engaging the audience in my own emotions and feelings. The score came alive through being authentic and totally in the flow of my intentions and appreciation of who I am while sincerely wanting to make a difference for others.

THE ART OF SPEAKING FEARLESSLY

I'm not sure how it all came together that I created Speaking Fearlessly™, except I was doing what I loved and was drawn to do. Instead of dancing like no one's watching, Speaking Fearlessly is, in a sense, just the opposite: speaking while *everyone* is watching and listening; connecting to and singing your message. Speaking *is* music — or it works best when it is.

Music has been a part of my life from the very beginning. I automatically memorized the melodies I heard, and by the age of three I was playing simple songs. When I check into my inner core, music is essential to my survival. Without it I am lost. It gives me rhythm, resonance, melody, and accompaniment — a full spectrum of sound expressed in equally individual notes. My brain and physiology are organized through the orchestration. I receive healing and well-being from the hormones produced when performing and listening. Interestingly, current research[*] finds music to be an intellectual reward by activating emotional processing regions of the brain "related to more willingness to drop some cash for a new song." And speaking is definitely like a song! Imagine: how can your presentation be scored to induce people to hire you or purchase your product?

I have a difficult time remembering words to music. This comes from a predominant fear of speaking well. My mind likes to wander off, images appear, worrying and judgments begin to strangle my thoughts — lots of stuff comes up that blocks my memorization. Also, the last thing I want to do is to practice when it seems easier to jump in and play around with something. But paradoxically it's the continued practice (playing with the script, exploring the voice and the emotions that are necessary

---

[*] Pappas, Stephanie. Music Purchases Predicted by Brain Activity. *Live Science. 11 April 2013. Retrieved on 7 September 2013 from http://www.livescience. com/28650-music-purchases-predicted-by-brain-activity.html.*

for it to resonate soundly and clearly) that makes it flow in an authentic and spontaneously congruent way.

Just a few weeks ago I was singing with a group of women, Harmony. I had the lead and my dream of backup singers. As the second verse came around I went totally blank. It could have been a horrible, shameful, embarrassing moment. I could have gone to a very frightening place — but I didn't. As I gave myself space, within seconds the words came and I gave a nod to the band to vamp one more time. I finished with flare.

A few years ago I would never have been able to do this. It is in the Speaking Fearlessly and Speaker Jams where I have developed my confidence, authenticity, and ability to think and create in the moment.

My vision of bringing the authentic nature of speakers into their presentations seems to have miraculously manifested. It wasn't really a vision, but more kinesthetic, intuitive, and very much in my body and senses. I had been holding speaking groups for three years when I met a remarkable woman, Sahar Kordahi, with a similar passion. She invited me to join her in a new venture, Voices of Leadership, and in just three and a half months we completed our first program. Entrepreneurs are voraciously looking for venues to speak and people to put them on stages. Our mission is to provide them that opportunity.

Voices of Leadership was resoundingly successful. Fifty people took part and 32 participated in an audition for six fifteen minute spots in the next event. We gave them tools, the stage, and opportunities to play full out. They loved it. We had telecalls, a stage, photographers, an image consultant, an audience, judges, and guest speakers. Voices of Leadership, with the Speaker Jams as a major component, was a huge success. The feeling of accomplishment that filled the room went far beyond our expectations. We saw this as powerfully instrumental in bringing out the leader in speakers to make a difference in our world and to give voice to their messages and gifts.

■ BECOMING A SUCCESSFUL SPEAKER

Speaking is one of the most effective ways to promote one's business, to get more clients and achieve results more quickly. But when you don't have the right score nothing much manifests. What makes a successful speaker? I believe there are two basic ingredients that must be in place and become automatic: authenticity and connection.

How do you get to that place where your emotions — the pain, the joy, the failures — can be shared in a way that connects you with potential clients? It takes practice and opportunity. I provide an absolutely safe practice environment that enables each participant to go beyond herself. Next, I offer the challenge to take action and risk the possibility (really the probability) of being awkward talking about personal stories, beliefs, experiences, and failures. The final piece is turning those imperfections into messages of transformation, healing, love, and offering them to others. These are the basics of a speaker's score. Anyone can learn them. Yes, *anyone*.

Life is a stage, a theatre where the spoken word is like a musical score. Without that score messages are lost or never even created, never performed, and never appreciated. Voices of Leadership and Speaker Jams offer the perfect stage for entrepreneurs to become masterful speakers who create much-needed communities for us all. I am so grateful to have a business partner who is also a friend who sees the same vision. Together we are inspired to bring more speakers to the stage.

It's time to create your score.

▓ *Meet the Contributor*

PAM WHITMAN, MA, is an entertaining, interactive and dynamic coach, international speaker and performer. She created Speaking Fearlessly™ and Speaker Jams to help transform speaking with fear and over-thinking presentations into communicating with the ease, confidence, and authenticity that brings success. Knowing that we learn best through pleasure, she employs her Brain Booster™ techniques to expertly unmask and nurture the natural way to establish a warm connection to any audience, either in person or through video. Pam received her music degree from Drake University and masters in holistic health from John F. Kennedy University. Her new DVD, *Better Balance & Brain Circuitry*, has just been released at www.brainboostersforboomers.com. She lives in Orinda, CA, and collaborates with Sahar Nefal Kordahi in the Voices of Leadership. Please contact Pam, the Speaking Fearlessly Coach, by email at info@transitionpoint.org or by phone at (925) 253-1223.

How to Become a Celebrity in Your Community

Mary Lou Luebbe-Gearhart (LBT #80)

"Those who bring sunshine to the lives of others
cannot keep it from themselves."
— *James Barrie*

I KNEW IT HAD HAPPENED when the emergency squad arrived at the scene of my accident. One of the paramedics said, "I recognize your voice. You're the hearing expert, Dr. Mary Lou." Then he sang my jingle, *Luebbe Hearing Services, you'll hear what you've been missing!* I had composed that in the key of A (for Audiology) on my piano at 5 a.m. one morning over twenty years ago. It was on the radio and TV. My slogan was in print. I was branded.

After I smiled and nodded my head, I felt so embarrassed because I had fallen and couldn't get up — just like that lady on the TV commercial. Then I realized there was a benefit to being "known," maybe even "beloved," in my city of one million people. Even though I literally "didn't have a leg to stand on" (having broken my left leg and right foot at the same time) I felt lucky. I felt a lot of pain, but mostly lucky.

▨ BECOMING A CELEBRITY

In a second I had lost my independence, my active lifestyle, and my mobility; but I knew there was a reason. I was to remain immobilized at home, away from my office, my employees, and my patients, living, eating, and sleeping in a La-Z-Boy recliner for five months. I depended on my canonized husband, "Saint" David, and the visiting home health care ladies who attended to my needs. Yet my faith reassured me that some purpose would become evident. I was forced to become more creative in order to exist. Life's funny like that. Once you realize and accept that this is going to be an amazing adventure or lesson, you can cope with anything and still be positive. That's the secret to living. You have to inspire yourself, as well as others. You have to be a good example because that holds you to a higher standard, while building character and celebrity.

Remember Jimmy Stewart in Capra's "It's a Wonderful Life"? The things he'd done during his life impacted others in various ways that weren't obvious to him. He was naturally helpful and kind. He wanted the best for others. He earned the trust and friendship of many people in his community. He became a "celebrity." That is, he became someone whose life should be "celebrated." He didn't realize how people felt about him until he hit hard times and needed their support.

I have experienced a similar realization as friends, business associates, patients, family members and neighbors sent flowers, home-cooked meals, cards, and prayers. I felt such love, appreciation, and spiritual uplifting from the care they showed me. I too had a chance to see how my life touched others. Was I on course? Were my life's goals the right ones? Did they involve something larger and more important than me? Every choice we make takes us in some direction. Every action we take and every word we use to communicate either weakens or strengthens our relationships, and eventually our community and nation.

▨ YOUR "WAKING" MOMENT

Have you ever wondered or tried to imagine how your funeral will be? Many ads for funeral homes impress upon us the importance of pre-planning. Some people avoid the topic and won't discuss it. Some pre-pay their expenses, decide where to put their remains, and even choose the flowers, music, and readings. But the truth is all of us unknowingly pre-plan our funerals every day of our lives through our conduct, values, and relationships.

My father used to tell me a person's "wake" (celebration of life) was literally what they left behind in the world. He equated this to the churned water waves (wake) left behind a sailing ship.

Ever thought of the environmental impact of your life? Like a passing ship, what are *you* leaving behind? How will it be when you're out of the picture?

In the last five months I've had a glimpse of what my wake would look like. For example, I could see how my amazing and dedicated staff worked even harder in my absence to maintain my business and keep my patients happy. I realized my business could run without me. What an epiphany! The right people, and the right systems to support them, enabled me to concentrate on my mission to fully recover.

What's your mission? Are you reaching your goals and realizing your dreams? Remember, as Ohio State football Coach Woody Hayes would say, "You win with people."

▨ CELEBRITY AND BUSINESS IS ALL ABOUT SERVING OTHERS

My accident was the second time in my life I had to overcome life-changing obstacles. You must believe your biggest and best opportunities are disguised as chaos, insurmountable odds, impossibilities, disappointments, and tragedies. Every tiny accomplishment in the face of your obstacles adds to your momentum and a "bring it on" attitude. Celebrities believe in themselves because they have gained confidence from successfully dealing with life's challenges. They develop courage, passion, talent, and networks of people (associations). If you continually say "yes" to requests, you will grow and learn and succeed because you have to.

My father, a pioneer in electronics, established our family business to help returning WWII veterans with noise-induced hearing loss. His brother, my Uncle Jim, also had a hearing loss. At age three, I remember how Dad was able to transform lives and restore communication with hearing aids. One day I saw a soldier crying in Dad's office. I asked my father, "Why?" He said, "Now he can hear again and that's what JOY looks like". I knew, at that young age, that I wanted to do the same for others. My father taught me about people. My mother taught me about following my dreams.

When my father died suddenly at age 58, I was still a student at Ohio State University. I took over the business and continued my education. My bachelor's degree is in business administration and marketing. My master's is in communication and audiology. I earned my doctorate in audiology at the University of Florida.

▨ CREATING SUCCESS FOR YOUR BUSINESS

Someone said that every baby comes into the world with a secret mission. Life and its challenges are so much easier if you know what your mission is. After almost forty years as president of my company, I have learned what it takes to succeed. You've got to know WHY you exist, WHAT you're here to do. Realize you'll also need to change and keep reinventing yourself so you can continue to accomplish your mission. What are YOU known for?

My parents believed in positive thinking. They were fans of Napoleon Hill and frequently consulted one of his books, *Think and Grow Rich*, to learn how to implement his principles for living. Life-long learning, self improvement, and being accountable and responsible were what they expected of themselves and of me.

You must earn people's respect, and they must earn yours. You've got to be your best self, all the time. That's congruity and authenticity.

You've got to be enthusiastic and have a winner's attitude. People appreciate it if you don't procrastinate. They want to get things done, too. At the end of the day, write down what you wanted to accomplish but didn't. Create your "to do" list and prioritize the items. When you organize at night, your subconscious gets "programmed" while you sleep. Just put a number in front of each item and complete each item in that order the next day. You'll get a lot more done because you thought it out and mapped it out the night before. This will accelerate your business because you will be able to accomplish more and delegate more. Take action.

Look for opportunities to be kind and non-judgmental. Have a thankful spirit and be appreciative and generous. Volunteer when you can. Do something unexpected and nice for someone every day. It forces you to be "tuned in" and creative. This will build your network. It may even be your "safety net(work)" one day.

Anticipate others' needs. My husband flew an F-4 Phantom in the Air Force. He learned to look a few miles ahead of the plane to avoid problems — little ones, and ones that could kill him.

In summary, think of the phrase, "PTA, Amen". Perhaps you remember the PTA (Parent Teachers Association) when you were in elementary school. It represented a unified approach to guide you to success in life. I use "P.T.A.A." to remind me of what is needed in order to be a celebrity: Passion, Talent, Associations, and Action. These are the desire, skills, people, and opportunities in your life to make a difference. Embrace them — and take action. People will notice.

■ *Meet the Contributor*

MARY LOU LUEBBE-GEARHART, AuD, is a board certified doctor of audiology and is recognized as one of America's most experienced and trusted hearing experts. She has served as president of Luebbe Hearing Services in Columbus, Ohio since 1973. Her passion for helping people hear what they've been missing has taken her around the world, using state of the art hearing aid technology to transform their lives. She is a charter member of the Women Presidents Organization (WPO) and serves on the board of trustees of People-to-People International. Go to www.hearohio.com to download your free gift, "A Guide to your Sound Experience." Contact her at drgearhart@columbus.rr.com.

TRANSITIONING TO SUCCESS

Donna Orbovich (LBT #87)

MANY OF US HAVE PAUSED and pondered, assessed and explored. We question the paths and choices we have made. Does this describe you? If so, you will inevitably come to a single conclusion throughout all of your self-evaluation: life is simply a series of experiences.

If further examined, this simple revelation will clarify itself even more: if our experiences are positive, joyful, and productive, then our lives will be positive, joyful, and productive. Likewise, if our experiences are agitating, so will our lives be agitated; if dull, numbness shall set into our existence; and if they are exciting, we will constantly be thrilled. This leads us to conclude that if we allow our experiences to be disconnected to any ideal or intention, we will have little chance of creating a shift or making a difference.

THE FORMULA FOR CHANGE

The formula for change in any life that is less than what you want it to be is simple — *change the experience to change the life*. What is not so simple (and what may appear to some as good fortune, but to others as hard work) is the "how to." Behind the "how to" is obviously the fear, the doubt, and the nagging worry that comes with thoughts of "What if I am not good enough to succeed, contribute, and change?"

For me, this massive question began forming during the year 2005, when I was in my eighth season as flutist with the Hong Kong Philharmonic. Somehow the experiences were no longer clicking; they had simply shown me all their tricks. What followed was an epiphany: I realized that finding happiness in my life was essentially up to me. It wasn't bound up in any job I held, concert I played, or praise I received.

Ever since I was a young teen, all I had wanted — or shall I say, all I'd *thought* I wanted — was to become a professional flutist. I worked hard at the conservatory I attended, went to various summer music festivals, and even attended a prestigious graduate school. I enjoyed my career, loved playing music, and carved out a dedication to the art that was impressive and, frankly, necessary to succeed in the classical music world.

It was easy to ride the waves of success, travel, and opportunity; but at some point my inner voice made a call home. I began to have fleeting ideas that there was more in life for me to explore. After a period of time, the thoughts were not so fleeting, and in fact took on a frequency that allowed them to be further analyzed.

▇ RECOGNIZING THE OPPORTUNITY

It all started when a friend encouraged me to attend a yoga class. She'd promised me it would be a wonderful exercise for both mind and body, spouting off all the health benefits that yoga has to offer. The studio itself was trendy and beautiful, and the classes were taught by professional teachers from India. It was a yogi's paradise.

And I hated it.

It was more like training for the circus instead of the simple running and swimming I was used to. But out of sheer determination, I stuck with it. As anyone who has practiced the art of yoga knows, it is very difficult for a cognitive shift not to occur when one is doing yoga. It's an awakening to one's subconscious pleas and requests, a dissection of past ideas and actions. We spend this peaceful time pondering our thoughts and feelings while we practice, and the shift begins to occur without us even knowing it.

My yoga-facilitated thoughts made me aware of my desire for a change. I was no longer energized by orchestral performance, and I was growing tired of living in a culture of materialism. I still had an inner drive, but I wondered how long I could keep it focused on just one aspect of my life. So in 2006 my daughter Zoe (who was eleven at the time) and I moved back to the United States. To protect my ability to earn income, I took a year off from the Philharmonic, and relocated to Grosse Pointe, MI, where I knew I could be helped by longtime friends to get work as a musician.

By the time the plane touched down in July, I knew that I was beginning a new chapter in my life. I reasoned that if I could strive, struggle, and succeed as a classical musician, I could start a business. As it turned out, that business would be a yoga studio! I was changing my experience to something that would change my life.

I took the hard work and dedication and went at it. Things began to fall into place, but there were still some roadblocks as I searched for the means and place to open my studio. Venues came and went. Landlords appeared willing to negotiate and then refused. At first, I couldn't figure out what was preventing this desire from shifting into action. So I once again returned to the formula and reexamined what kind of experience I was trying to create.

What surfaced was that my actions were originating from a selfish place. I had experienced burnout in the music business, and a part of me wanted to retreat, to not connect to any person or ideal. What I really wanted right then was to check out. This was masquerading beautifully as a desire to open a yoga studio. However, that goal would not come to fruition until one thing settled in its place, and that was an Ideal.

▪ A SHIFT TOWARD SUCCESS

The shift came after many conversations with people who shared their own personal experiences with success and failure. This allowed me a greater understanding of the pain that often surrounds individuals and a realization of the lack of appreciation many people have for the tools we organically have rights to. Over a period of months, my obsession to make a difference in peoples' lives and the world allowed for a shift in energy of the project. Once I fully understood what this amazing thing called yoga could do for people, and how I could bring it into the lives of others, everything fell into place. The fear was replaced with confidence and a desire to serve. Energy and enthusiasm grew from the concept of being of service. With this inner shift, help came to me at the right time.

And without my even realizing it, a community blossomed. People came in for classes, made friends, created spaces, and grew strong in body and mind. All of this inspired me to try to lead by example, to serve yet understand the art of creating energetic boundaries. I began to gain an understanding of unity within diversity — the oneness connection, so to speak. Once realized, the potential for this to successfully propel any business forward is limitless.

It was all simply a shift in thinking, transitioning from a small and selfish game to a large and spirited playing field. I am grateful to have had mentors who helped me change my mental patterns and see the big picture even before the small pieces fell into place. This willingness to change experiences and play a bigger role is essential in becoming an entrepreneur!

▨ Meet the Contributor

DONNA ORBOVICH spent most of her life as a classical flutist until she opened her first yoga studio in 2008. She lives with her partner, Nick, and travels frequently to India to visit her daughter, who is a student at NYUAD. Donna is a professional speaker and Breakthrough Leadership Coach who finds meaning in the words of Steve Jobs: "Our time here is limited, so let's not waste it living someone else's life." You can contact Donna at www.authenticthoughts.com.

40 YEAR JOURNEY TO SUCCESS: PERSISTENCE WINS THE DAY

Craig Batley (LBT #90)

MY MOTHER AND FATHER raised us four kids during the 1950s and early 1960s. It was a simpler time, a time when kids used their imagination and ingenuity to play and have fun in neighborhoods with unlocked doors and a carefree environment. My parents were children during the Great Depression, a hard school where you learned to pay cash for everything; if you borrowed tools you returned them in better condition than when you found them, and you respected your elders. The people of that generation took pride in being self-sufficient, independent, and thrifty.

My father was the epitome of the Greatest Generation: Self-reliant, industrious and honest. He loved his family. Discipline, hard work, and satisfaction in a job well done were the values he and my mother instilled in their children. Those principles were the seeds my parents planted for my future success. All I had to do was learn how to put them to work. I mowed yards in the summer, had a paper route and collected the subscription fees from my customers every month, and worked at a service station for $1.50/hour. I saved my money and traveled to Europe and the Soviet Bloc countries during the summer prior to my freshman year at the University of Washington.

Ours was a middle class family. My dad never took much time off work. I was 12 years old when we took our one family vacation: my grandparents drove me and my three sisters to La Jolla, California, for a glorious two weeks at the beach and a visit to Disneyland. This was the first time that I experienced something outside my familiar world, and it made a lasting impression on me. The contrast between Seattle and Southern California was more than geography — it was an attitude of "opportunity thinking." I wanted more.

I had the good fortune of meeting three successful businessmen during my teenage years. These businessmen took a liking to me and shared their wisdom and insight, giving me a window into their success. I dreamed of becoming a successful businessman, or maybe a salesman. I later learned you have to be both. Unlike my father who was a dedicated engineer at Boeing for 40 years where he earned a pension, these mentors were independent entrepreneurial businessmen.

After graduation with a BA in business administration, and two years later an MBA emphasizing entrepreneurship, I was ready to interview for a career with an eye for future success. After five interviews and personality profile testing as a prerequisite to work for a national real estate brokerage company, HR informed me that, yes, I was an ambitious young man, but I was not a fit for them, being a bit too impetuous for their program. This was a major setback, but, undaunted, I interviewed with Standard Oil for a two year training program designed especially for MBAs. During the interview they offered me an attractive starting salary. Being curious as to what my future would look like if I accepted, I asked, "Approximately what may I expect my salary to be five years from now?" They thumbed through the pages of a large binder and looked up exactly what they projected my salary to be in five years and proudly announced, "You will be making the tidy sum of $2,345 per month; three times the starting salary."

I knew right then and there that the corporate world was not for me. I didn't want my future salary to be dictated or limited by bean counters. I wanted pay commensurate to my income-producing performance. I remembered another mentor, Bob Bebee, who quit his corporate job as the most productive, highest-paid salesman for SCM Corporation to become an entrepreneur, going on to earn three times what he was earning as the top salesman in a 1,000+ sales-force.

One of my early mentors, Frank Satter, told me, "You get what you ask for in life." I didn't fully understand what he meant until years later, but I knew my parents were not going to hand me the silver spoon. I decided to follow my heart (listening to that "still small voice"), and struck out on my own. I didn't know what I was going to do, but I knew whatever it was it would be good and I would be living in Southern California.

Sometimes we don't know the ultimate destination, but our journey begins with that first step of faith. I had a yearning desire (not quite burning yet, but beginning to smolder) to break free from the yoke of predictability and family expectations. I decided to pursue possibility thinking instead of probability thinking. In 1972 I made the decision to pack up and move to Southern California, the land of opportunity. I moved from the Pacific Northwest and secured a sales-rep job with a small distributor of building products. The job was to be a stepping stone to future possibilities. The day I met my boss, I knew I was going to quit and pursue my goal of being an entrepreneur. However, because I had the courage to take the leap of faith and seek new opportunity, my then-boss did me a huge favor and suggested I might enjoy living at the Oakwood Garden Apartments in Newport Beach. I took that suggestion, and it was there that I met my next mentor and employer, a successful independent millionaire entrepreneur named Rudy. Rudy taught me how to make cold calls, an invaluable business sales skill. He made me realize that I had to unlearn many of the skills and preconceived notions I had garnered growing up and during my years in business school. I had to unlearn many of the conventional ideas that had shaped my view of the world in order to learn the skill set of becoming a successful entrepreneur.

After two years of apprenticeship with Rudy, I ventured out on my own in 1977 as a novice flipper of real estate. I started buying and selling houses and small income properties. I rehabbed a property and sold it six months later for a profit of $42,000, just by making a phone call. Of course, I had made dozens of phone calls before I found that one willing seller. You never know what the next call will bring until you make the call.

It was my desire to achieve my goal of becoming a millionaire through real estate investing. I was well on my way — the proud owner of a dozen properties. However, in 1978 I stopped listening to that "still small voice" and took a 13-year detour when I made the decision to pioneer the 100- percent commission concept by opening the first RE/MAX office in California. The offices I opened were very successful, but I allowed myself to get into debt. Fortunately, I foresaw the coming recession and unloaded my thriving, but marginally profitable, multimillion dollar company in 1991. I consolidated my four sales offices into one mega Newport Beach office and sold at a fire sale price. After paying off debt there wasn't much left. I was no longer a millionaire and had to start over.

After nearly 20 years of being the broker of a large company that closed thousands of real estate transactions and employed a few hundred real estate agents, I was just able to pay off my debts with enough left over to live on for a few years while I contemplated what to do for my next career move. After several years of self-reflection and working solo, I decided to stay in the real estate business. I was beginning to learn that if you listen to that "still small voice" or that "whisper in your ear" before making decisions, good results always occur. I decided to enter the arena of property management, a cash flow business. After 20 years, I had come to realize property management was a much better fit for me.

With a partner, I bought a small company in 1997 on the Balboa Peninsula in Newport Beach that had been in business continuously in the same location for 30 years. At that time, Burr White Realty managed about 65 "doors," including houses and duplexes. About half of them were vacation rentals. Almost 16 years later the business has grown 800 percent and we own the property on which the business began 46 years ago. Burr White Realty is now positioned to move to the next level. In the next few years, using my experience, expertise, and innovative services, I intend to expand our scope of operations beyond Newport Beach into Orange County via merger and acquisitions.

What are the lessons to be learned from my 40 years as an entrepreneur?

The five basic lessons I learned to become a successful entrepreneur are:

* **Never, ever go into personal debt.** The 10 percent SBA loan I took out in 1979 ballooned to 23.5 percent (3 percent over prime) in January 1982 when prime was 20.5 percent. It is not wise to borrow your way to success. Does that mean you cannot sell equity shares in your company? No. Does that mean you should not seek venture capital? No. There are exceptions, but in general I recommend not being personally liable for business debt. Instead, grow organically. Grow your company to success. Use the profits of the business to expand. If the product you offer is in demand, sell it and keep on selling it over and over until the cash flow creates profit. Until your company has a record of increasing sales and generating a profit, it is difficult to attract investment capital.

* **Especially in the beginning, learn to ask for the order.** Sell your product 24/7. When your business is in its infancy, you as an owner are the best salesman for your product. Most likely, during startup you cannot afford to hire sales people. If you cannot sell your product, who can? Become your company's best advocate for your product or service. Believe what you have to offer is the best in the marketplace. And when selling, remember to take the advice of my mentor, Bob Bebee. The best sales advice I ever received was when he said, "don't say ugh, ugh, when ugh will do."

* **Be persistent.** Persistence wins the prize every time. Never give up. Believe you have the best product or service. Make dozens of calls a day. Sell, then sell some more.

* **Hire good people.** Hire employees who are team players. Hire people who believe in you, who compliment your skills, are enthusiastic and want the company to be successful.

* **In this technological world we live in, we must innovate and stay ahead of the competition.** It doesn't matter if your competitors copy you, because by the time they figure out how to do what you

are doing, you will have graduated to the next level, staying at least one or two steps ahead of your competitors.

I became an "overnight" success after 40 years by dogged determination and overcoming all the obstacles and setbacks that seemingly block the road to all those who seek success. Success is something you grow into after learning from your own mistakes. I made hundreds of mistakes along the way. At this stage of my life, new business opportunities occur because of the expertise garnered through some modicum of success. I can now distinguish a genuine opportunity from an ephemeral one.

Remember, success can be just around the corner; it can be the next phone call or next appointment. Do not procrastinate. Make that phone call today.

■ *Meet the Contributor*

Since 1997, CRAIG BATLEY and his partner have managed Burr White Realty, a full-service boutique real estate office. The longevity and recognition Burr White Realty enjoys has not been achieved easily or by accident. The rewards of honesty, integrity, and loyalty have been hard-earned by providing consistent quality, value, and service to each and every client. Today on the Balboa Peninsula, Burr White Realty maintains its reputation with its long-held clients as the area's most capable property manager, specializing in vacation rentals, property management, and sales. You may view the website at www.newportbeachvactionrentals.com . Craig invites you to visit the beach at Newport Beach, his home these past 40 years.

FINISH IT:
MAKING IT TO CLOSURE IN A WORLD OF ADD

Marion O'Malley (LBT #87)

"Knowing you need to make a change isn't enough.
You've got to find the guts to do it!"
— Robert Kyosaki

"Go CATCH A BUTTERFLY." My mother remembered sending me on this unorthodox errand to give her some grown-up time with her friends. I was just five years old.

"And then damned if you didn't just skedaddle over to the bushes and pluck one out of thin air. Brought it back in two minutes flat, the yellow of its wings still on your fingers."

So I wasn't always a procrastinator. I was born knowing how to do things: quickly and deliberately, with focus and determination.

I'm not sure when that changed. Was it because, as a lifelong educator, I grew comfortable planting seeds and never really knowing if they'd taken root and sprouted unless I later saw a student who said how much my note-taking class had saved his life in college? I don't really know. I simply trusted.

I'm a P on the Myers Briggs personality test — a Perceiver rather than a J (Judger). Judgers like closure: making a decision, taking a left or a right, closing the deal. In contrast, I could watch the tennis game of life all day long. I am a creative type, and dislike pinning myself down or focusing on only a single thing when there are so many delicacies in the candy store waiting to be sampled. I like being my own boss, setting my own schedule, being able to switch and change activities at will. Why limit myself?

Little did I know — I *was* limiting myself.

Once, in an otherwise pleasant party conversation, some young whippersnapper interrupted me and said, "Oh you must be ADHD."

I recoiled. Who was she to call me that? Had she started a Center for Peace Education, helped build a house with her very own hands, written a great book on dealing with differences, had three kids, *and* taught exceptional children for 20 years? Even if I was "ADH" (attention deficit hyperactive), I certainly wasn't "D" (disorder). I just *wasn't* a linear thinker, that's all.

The discovery that I wasn't reaching my full potential only came when I attended my first session of Loral's Big Table. Loral quickly looked at my multitude of coincidental projects and said, "Oh you have a horizontal model."

No judgment — just the facts, ma'am. I had a horizontal model. Put another way, if I ever wanted to finish things and make some money, I had to have a vertical model.

Leaders are known for starting things. But successful leaders actually *FINISH* the things they start. I've been fortunate enough to study this behavior in entrepreneurs the world over, and my challenge to you is to make this year "The Year of Finishing Things." If you're up for that challenge, I'd like to complete this chapter by sharing with you the insights I've learned by interviewing successful entrepreneurs in multiple countries. The methods they use to "finish things" have many common elements — see how many you can discover!

Oh, and one last note: a few of these people were born finishers, but most were not! You, too, can acquire this skill.

▨ Step 1: Create a Compelling Vision

Create a *clear* and *compelling* vision for your life and your business that produces *excitement* and a sense of *possibility*. This is the foundation. Most people don't have a vision that is compelling enough. It should be a BIG STRETCH — maybe a bit scary, barely believable. This shifts your focus from all the petty problems and distractions that surround you. The entrepreneurs I interviewed offered these thoughts about compelling visions:

"Once I have a vision, I keep coming back to it. My business coach taught me to get everything out of my head and onto paper, to document my vision. This really makes a difference. It raises my level of consciousness about what I'm doing."

"I am good at getting it done when I have a crystal clear goal that completes me."

"Separate the vision from the 'how.' *The 'how' will come later.*"

"I learned not to flounder around without a plot."

▨ Step 2: Create a Plan

Develop a blueprint. Make it specific. Put it on a calendar. Follow it.

"I take an inordinate amount of time to learn everything about the topic. Then I plan how I will implement that learning. I put it on a calendar: *how I am going to roll it out. Only then do I implement.*"

"Every day I think, 'What are the Five Biggest Rocks?' I lift the Big Rocks first. It might take me only 'til 11 in the morning, but I lift the big ones first."

"Think of the larger goal first. Every day. Come back to your vision. Then break it down into the next three things you need to do to get it done. Carve out time in your schedule, and learn to say 'No' to things that are not going to support it getting done."

"I told myself to write for an hour every day, Monday thru Friday. *I could write longer if I wanted but I must write an hour. I could work on weekends, but I didn't have to. And I gave myself five 'sick days or well days' for the year — days in which I could blow it off without feeling like I was breaking a pact with myself, without letting myself down. I think this was very important, because once you decide to do something and then don't do it one day, it can have a snowball effect."*

◻ Step 3: Consider the Backdrop

Atmospherics count: time of day, materials, environmental setting, background music — whatever makes it easier for you to work. Arrange your life. Don't just leave this all to chance.

"I already knew that I was a morning person, that my energy and attitude was always best at the beginning of the day, so I decided to try that. *I set the alarm an hour early and I wrote before I went to work, and it turned out that I loved it. I loved being awake before dawn. I loved going to bed early at night. It fit with my biorhythms better than anything I'd tried. There was an added benefit in that I was working closer to my dream state, closer to my subconscious, at a time of day when I had the least resistance to it."*

"I advise giving it your best hours of the day, the hours that you feel the most energetic and clear. *Give yourself a room if you can, a desk where you can leave your work out, a place that you do not have to share, not just with other people, but with other tasks like bill paying and balancing the checkbook. If you can afford it, get a computer that is solely for this, so that Facebook energy and email energy do not bleed onto your canvas. Keep it sacred. Draw boundaries with the people you live with. If you don't respect the boundaries you draw, no one else will either."*

◻ Step 4: Get a Team

Even if you are a writer requiring lots of solitary time, you need a team. Start with a housecleaner. Loral taught me this. Being a "solopreneur" is for the birds; maybe obsessive, a little megalomaniacal, certainly slow. You're not good at everything. Only do what you're good at and like. Hire out the rest!

"When I have a team behind me, I do much better. I interact with my team, include them in the vision, why it will make a difference, then let them go. For me a team is essential."

"Bookkeeper, accountant, folks to help with operational things that are ongoing and hard and that they are better at anyway. Automate as much as possible!"

"The once-a-week Mastermind Team is my lifeline and my life-saver."

"Get a consultant. Spend the money and work with a professional, someone who's been where you want to go."

"My problem may be I am too collaborative, too social. I put out a lot of energy for other people. I need to say 'NO' more, stop and assess what it's going to take before I commit. A part of it is about conserving my energy and focusing. I think I have a boundless amount. I don't."

▨ Step 5: Know Yourself

It's important to know both your strengths and your weaknesses.

"I have to set daily goals. I know my weaknesses, and one of them at the moment is getting things finished. I have more ideas than I have time or resources to fill. I ask myself each morning: What have I started that I have not finished? How can I move this forward today?"

"Once when I was having trouble with discipline, I bemoaned this to a friend, and she said *'You have to get aggressive with it.' I don't think she knows what a difference that change in language made for me. Discipline was something that had always been done to me. Aggression was something I could take control of. I never forgot that.*"

A few other pearls of great wisdom from my enterprising friends:

* **Break the project down into smaller pieces.** To be more productive and remain motivated to finish the project, you have to break it into smaller, more manageable portions. Then it will not seem so daunting. What's more, as you complete one step and before you go to the next, you will have a sense of satisfaction, a sense of accomplishment, which feels wonderful, psychologically. This alone will motivate you to move to the next task.

- **Apply the 80/20 Rule.** Stop making excuses or just reaching for whatever's top of your pile. Do the 20 percent that will get 80 percent of the results. For example, find that model company doing what you want to be doing and make an appointment to interview the CEO rather than organize your filing drawer. Create momentum.

- **Drop perfectionism.** Good enough is good enough. Launch it, even sell it, before you know how you're going to do it. Remember, HOW comes later.

- **Perseverance pays!** Don't be so quick to judge the outcome or decide it's not going to work. Find your passion and begin to work on it. Maybe you don't see results quickly: perhaps your wallet's no thicker or you don't know how much longer you have to wait until it is. What most of us miss in this process are the huge changes taking place inside of us, changes we're so close to we can't see them ourselves. Trust the process — you may be just inches from the vein of gold. Keep going!

- **Celebrate.** Be nice and give yourself a reward. Take breaks. Seriously, take breaks! Get OFF-task! Once the celebration is over, go back and finish off another task. Notice the difference in your mood. You will be more productive than before, and you will feel more motivated to work. Laugh often. Find joy in the process, not just the completion. Find pleasure in everything you do as much as humanly possible. It's not just your passion or your business. It's your life.

For some of us, the thing holding us back may be bad habits or the feeling we don't have the know-how or the money to move from our starting point to the finish line. However, it's always good to be aware of the psychology behind procrastination: chronic delaying because of fears or insecurities. Experts say 20 percent of us experience this. Whether the problem is task avoidance, fears of inadequacy, or feeling indecisive, we can all learn to change this behavior.

Non-procrastinators focus on the task that needs to be done. They have a stronger personal identity and are less concerned about what psychologists call "social esteem" — how others like them — as opposed to self-esteem, which is how they feel about themselves. There's a long literature available for further research.

But don't research too long. That's just stirring the soup. Go for the finish line.

If you pick just a few of these tools shared by my intrepid contributors, they will dramatically improve your batting average of completed projects. In closing, I offer these universal mantras: "No one is going to do it for you." and "You can fix it later." Remember — unless you do something start to finish, your dream will always remain a dream!

Meet the Contributor

MARION O'MALLEY is an educator, entrepreneur, life coach, and author. Her published books include *Dealing with Differences: A Training Manual for Young People and Adults on Intergroup Relations, Diversity, and Multicultural Education; Two Dates a Week: Rekindling the Spark* (www.twodatesaweekworks. com), written with her husband; and her upcoming memoir, *Shopping with Mama.*

Marion is currently finishing two works of fiction: one set along the NC coast, *Serenity Point,* and the other along the Ecuadorian coast where she has a beach house, *Playa Majica.* When not traveling, she lives with her husband and cats in North Carolina and engages with her children and grandchildren every chance she gets. For this chapter, in addition to her own ideas, Marion interviewed Laena Wilder, photographer extraordinaire from San Francisco; Nancy Peacock, an amazing author from North Carolina; and Tracey Thomson, founder of an Australian company specializing in manufacturing organic skin care products. Contact Marion at marionwomalley@gmail.com.